PHP

I0014577

Beginner's Practical Guide

by

BPB PUBLICATIONS
20 Ansari Road, Darya Ganj New Delhi-110002

FIRST EDITION 2018

ISBN: 978-93-8728-420-3

publishers.

LIMITS OF LIABILITY AND DISCLAIMER OF WARRANTY

The Author and Publisher of this book have tried their best to ensure that the programmes,

the publishers make no warranty of any kind, expressed or implied, with regard to these

or arising out of the furnishing, performance or use of these programmes, procedures and

owners.

Distributors:

BPB PUBLICATIONS
20, Ansari Road, Darya Ganj
New Delhi-110002
Ph: 23254990/23254991

DECCAN AGENCIES
4-3-329, Bank Street,
Hyderabad-500195
Ph: 24756967/24756400

COMPUTER BOOK CENTRE
12, Shrungar Shopping Centre,
M.G.Road, BENGALURU–560001
Ph: 25587923/25584641

BPB BOOK CENTRE
376 Old Lajpat Rai Market,
Delhi-110006
Ph: 23861747

MICRO MEDIA
Shop No. 5, Mahendra Chambers, 150
DN Rd. Next to Capital Cinema, V.T.

22078296/22078297

Delhi-110002 and Printed by Repro India Ltd., Mumbai

Preface

The author is confident that the present work will come as a relief to the students wishing to go through a comprehensive work explaining the programming concepts through examples with proper description, offering a variety of practical examples and conceptual problems along with their systematically worked out solutions and to top of it, covering all the concepts which are helpful for students to learn basics of php and develop projects using it.

This book promises to be a very good starting point for beginners and an asset for those having insight towards programming.

This book is written taking into consideration the skills required at beginner level for developing websites starting from the HTML to php with MySQL. The book covers the practical examples of php in an easy way, so that students can able to understand in an efficient manner.

It is said "To err is human, to forgive divine". Although the book is written with sincerity and honesty but in this light I wish that the shortcomings of the book will be forgiven. At the same the author is open to any kind of constructive criticisms and suggestions for further improvement. All intelligent suggestions are welcome and the author will try it's best to incorporate such in valuable suggestions in the subsequent editions of this book.

Acknowledgement

No task is a single man's effort. Cooperation and Coordination of various peoples at different levels go into successful implementation of this book. There is always a sense of gratitude, which every one expresses others for their helpful and needly services they render during difficult phases of life and to achieve the goal already set.

At the outset I am thankful to the almighty who is constantly and invisibly guiding and have also helped me to work on the right path.

I am very much thankful to my parents and family for their guidance which motivated me to work for the betterment of students by writing the book with sincerity and honesty. Without their support, this book is not possible.

I wish my sincere thanks to colleagues who helped and kept me motivated for writing this text.

I also thank the Publisher and the whole staff at BPB Publications, especially **Mr. Manish Jain** for motivation and for bringing this text in a nice presentable form.

Finally, I thank everyone who has directly or indirectly contributed to complete this authentic work.

Table of contents

Chapter 11 Object Oriented Programming

Chapter 12 Regular Expressions and PDO Fundamentals

Appendix- A

APPENDIX-B

Chapter 1

Introduction

1.1 What is HTML?

HTML is Hypertext Markup Language which runs on a client machine having web browser installed in it.

It is invented by Tim-Berners Lee for the Internet.

HTML is Tag-based language which can be written on notepad or any other web-based editors like Dreamweaver, Notepad++ etc.

Every HTML Document should contain tags which are the elements and attributes associated with the tag.

Static websites are developed in HTML whereas for dynamic websites, languages like Asp.Net, PHP, Java Server Pages (JSP) etc. are used.

In HTML, there are opening and closing tags. The opening tags is <html> and closing tag is </html>.

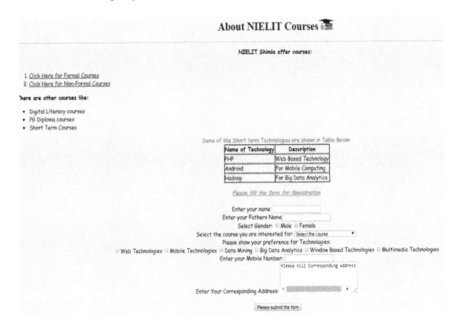

Fig.1.1: Webpage Designed using HTML Tags

Here, a webpage is shown in Figure 1.1, is designed by using commonly used HTML Tags. These tags are discussed in Example 1.1.

The tags mentioned in Example 1.1 are described in Table 1.1

Tags used	Description
<html>	Starting tag of the web page document.
<head> </head>	Inside <head>tag, JavaScript programs are embedded.
<title> </title>	<title> tag is used to give title to the web page
<body>	HTML document which will be visible on the web page.
<h1> <h2> <h3>	These tags are used for Heading
<p align="center">	Paragraph tag and for center alignment attribute "align is used"
<img src = "img.jpg" width = "50" height="30">	<img> tag is for displaying the image.
<b> <i> <u>	<b> means bold, <i> means italic, <u> means underline
<hr> 	It is used for giving horizontal row break tag is used to move to next line whereas tag is used to give whitespaces.
<font face = "Comic Sans MS" color = "Black">	This is font tag used for selecting font family, size of font and color.
<ol> <li>Ordered list</li> </ol> <ul> <li>unordered list</li> </ul>	Here "ol" means ordered list and "ul" means unordered list and "li" means list item.
<a href="formal.html">Click Here for Formal Courses</a>	This tag is used for hyperlink to another page. Here <a> means "anchor tag"
<table border = "1" align ="center"> <tr>	This tag is known as Table tag and is used for providing information in Tabular format.
<th>Name of Technology</th> <th>Description</th> </tr> <tr> <td>PHP</td> <td>Web Based Technology</td> </tr></table>	<tr> means table row, <th> means table heading and <td> means table data. The <tr> tag is closed with </tr> and same is the case with <th> and <td>
Enter your name <input type = "text"	and name is the attribute for passing parameters which are used in JavaScript and PHP.

Select Gender:

```
<input type = "radio" name = "gender"
value ="M">Male
```
radio buttons.

```
<input type = "radio" name = "gender"
value ="F">Female
```

Select the course you are interested for:

This tag is used for displaying dropdown list. For this tag, we use

```
<select name = "menu">
<option>Select the course</option>
<option>Non-Formal Courses
</option>
<option>Formal Courses</option>
<option>Industrial Courses</option>
<option>Short Term Training Program
</ option>
</select>
```

```
<select name=" menu"><option>A</option>
<option>B</option>
</select>
```

Please show your preference for Technologies:

```
<br>
<input type ="checkbox"
name="Web">Web Technologies
<input type = "checkbox"
name="Mobile">Mobile Technologies
<input type ="checkbox"
name="Mining">Data Mining
```

`<input type ="checkbox">` tag is used for displaying checkboxes.

one item is selected whereas in

selected.

Enter Your Corresponding Address:

`<textarea name= "address" rows="5" cols="30">`

```
<textarea name = "address" rows="5"
cols="30">
Please Fill Corresponding Address </
textarea>
```

cols. This tag is used where more description is required in place of simple textboxes.

```
<input type = "submit" value="Please
submit the form">
```
This tag is used to display the submit button.

also<HTML>

Example 1.1 HTML Tags

```
<html>
<head>
</head>
<title>Example of HTML</title>
```

```
<body bgcolor="#FCF3CF">
<h1 color="#050E3C" align = "center"> About NIELIT Courses<img src = "img.jpg"
width = "50" height="30"> </h1>


<hr color = "orange">
<p align = "center">
<font face = "Comic Sans MS" color = "Black" >

<br>
           &nb
sp;
<ol>
<li> <a href="formal.html">Click Here for Formal Courses</a> </li>
<li> <a href="nonformal.html">Click Here for Non-Formal Courses</a> </li>
</ol>

<b>There are other courses like:</b>
           &nb
sp;
<ul>
<li>Digital Literacy courses</li>
<li>PG Diploma courses</li>
<li>Short Term Courses</li>
</ul>


</p>
<p align="center"><font face = "Comic Sans MS" color = "#F70425">Some of the
Short term Technologies are shown in Table Below:</font> <br>
<table border = "1" align ="center">
<tr>
<th>Name of Technology</th>
<th>Description</th>
</tr>

<tr>
<td>PHP</td>
<td>Web Based Technology</td>
</tr>
```

```
<tr>
<td>Android</td>
<td>For Mobile Computing</td>
</tr>

<tr>
<td>Hadoop</td>
<td>For Big Data Analytics</td>
</tr>
</table>

<p align = "center"><b><i><u><font face = "Comic Sans MS" color = "#F97915"

<br><br>

<br>
Enter your Father's Name<input type = "text" name = "fname">
<br>
Select Gender:
<input type = "radio" name = "gender" value ="M">Male
<input type = "radio" name = "gender" value ="F">Female
<br>
Select the course you are interested for:

<select name = "menu">
<option>Select the course</option>
<option>Non-Formal Courses</option>
<option>Formal Courses</option>
<option>Industrial Courses</option>
<option>Short Term Training Program</option>
</select>
<br>
Please show your preference for Technologies:
<br>
<input type = "checkbox" name="Web">Web Technologies
<input type = "checkbox" name="Mobile">Mobile Technologies
```

```
<input type = "checkbox" name="Mining">Data Mining
<input type = "checkbox" name="BigData">Big Data Analytics
<input type = "checkbox" name="Windows">Window Based Technologies
<input type = "checkbox" name="Multimedia">Multimedia Technologies
<br>
Enter your Mobile Number:
<input type="text" name="mobile">
<br>
Enter Your Corresponding Address:

<textarea name = "address" rows="5" cols="30">
Please Fill Corresponding Address
</textarea>

<br>
<br>
<input type = "submit" value="Please submit the form">
</p>
</body>
</html>
```

1.2 What is PHP?

PHP: Hypertext Preprocessor is a widely-used open source general-purpose scripting language that is especially suited for web development and can be embedded into HTML.

PHP is:

  Server-side Scripting Language.

  Runs on Server-side not on client side.

  Client going to be user's browser.

  Need not to be compiled like other languages.

  Designed for use with HTML.

   PHP code is input and web pages are output.

   Syntax similar to Perl.

1.2.1 History of PHP

PHP was developed in 1994 by Rasmus Lerdorf and was a set of CGI (Common Gateway Interface) binaries written in the C Programming Language.

Version 1: In 1994: CGI Binaries in C Programming Language.

Version 2: In 1995: "Personal Home Page Tools".

Version 3: In 1998: "Hypertext Preprocessor".

Version 4: In 2000: still actively supported by updates.

Version 4.4.6 on March 1, 2007.

Version 5.2.1 on February 8,2007, provides OOPs and embedded database.

Latest Version of PHP is 7.0.0.

1.2.2 How to Run PHP Programs?

In order to run PHP Programs,wamp or xampp servers can be used. In these servers, all the software's which run PHP programs are bundled together and which results in

WampServer is a Windows web development environment and open source project. It consists of Apache, PHP and a MySQL database. Along with it, PhpMyAdmin allows to manage databases. Wampserver can be downloaded from http://www.wampserver. com/

1.2.3 Installing WampServer

WampServer can be downloaded from the website www.wampserver.com. Here the examples of PHP are run with the help of WampServer. Figure 1.2, shows that the Wampserver is installed in C: \wamp drive location.

Saving PHP Files :

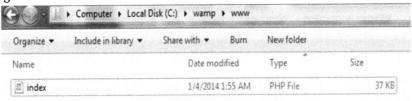

Figure 1.2:

PHP programs can be written in simple notepad or there are editors like Dreamweaver, notepad++ which can be used for writing the PHP programs as these software provide GUI based environment for writing programs. In Example 1.2, PHP program is written along with HTML i.e. Hypertext Markup Language which is tag based and with help of HTML, static websites are developed whereas for Dynamic Websites PHP,

Asp.Net, JSP like Web based languages are followed.

Example 1.2

```
<html>
<head>
<title>
My First Page in Php
</title>
<body bgcolor = "Black">
<font color = "White">
<?php

  echo "Welcome in Php World";

?>
</font>
</body>
</html>
```

✓ The example 1.2 shows the syntax of PHP program where only message is displayed with the help of echo keyword.

Where to save PHP program shown in Example 1.2?

Whenever we create a new PHP page, we need to save it in WWW directory.

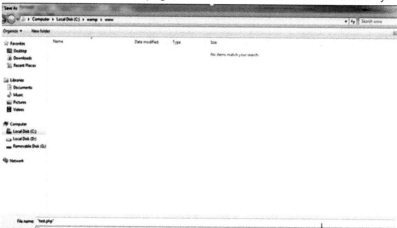

Figure.1.3: Location of PHP Program. Here the name of program shown in Example 1.1 is saved with "test.php"

The location of www folder for WampServer is usually: c:\wamp\www. The program shown in Example 1.2 is to be saved in location "C:\wamp\www\create your own folder\test.php. While saving this program in Notepad, the extension of program will be ".php" and character set will be UTF-8.

Run PHP Program on local host:

The program shown in Example 1.2 show the output on web page by following the following steps:

✓ To run the php program, first start the services of Wamp server by clicking the shortcut of Wamp on Desktop shown in Figure 1.4.

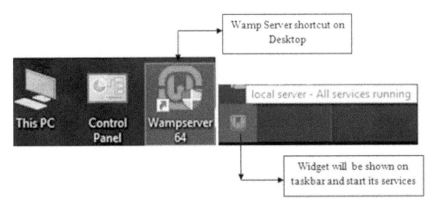

Figure 1.4: Starting services of WampServer

✓ After following this step, click the browser either Chrome or Internet explorer and type in URL the path of PHP program i.e. the local host. The location of PHP program is C:\Wamp\www\create your own folder\ filename.php. HereFigure 1.5 shows the default page of WampServer i.e. index.php if server is installed successfully.

✓ When the URL address is given by the client, then the Apache Server serve the request and find the PHP page, if the page having .php extension is available on server, then the request is fulfilled and page will be responded to client. The Client-server communication for finding PHP page on Apache server is shown in Figure.1.6

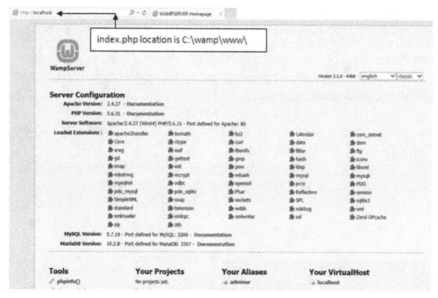

Figure 1.5: Running Php Program on localhost

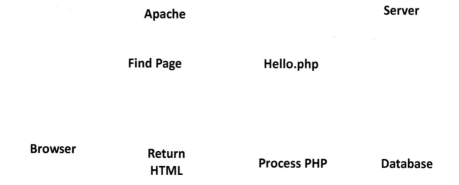

Figure 1.6: Client-Server Communication while processing of PHP Page

In PHP by default local host is running on port no.80 but in case the same port is being used by some another application or IIS server, then the port address is to be

Listen 0.0.0.0:79
Listen [::0]:79
ServerName localhost:79

Figure 1.7:

CHAPTER 2

Variable Declaration

2.1 What is variable?

The variables are containers for storing information. In PHP variable starts with the $ sign, followed by the name of the variable.

Note: PHP variables are case-sensitive

Variables in PHP:

Starts with a $.
Followed by an underscore or letter.
Can contain letters, underscores, or dashes.
Variable name cannot start with a number no spaces.
case-sensitive.

Example of Variable Declaration:

Example 2.1

```php
<? php
  $name = "Pratiyush Guleria";// variable declaration
  ?>

<html>
<head>
<title>Variables </title>
</head>
<body>
<p>
<strong>
```

<!-- print variable name's value -->

```php
        Welcome to PHP, <?php print( "$name" ); ?>!
</strong>
</p>
</body>
</html>
```

Example 2.2

```php
<?php
$message = "containers for data storage";
echo "Variables are $message";
```

?>

The example 2.2 can also be written as shown in Example 2.3. In Example 2.3, the output obtained is same but here, the variable is concatenated to string with dot symbol.

Example 2.3

```php
<?php
$message = "containers for data storage";
echo "variables are=" .$message."Please Read";
?>
```

Example 2.4: Addition of Integer values

```php
<?php
$num1 = 5;
$num2 = 4;
echo $num1 + $num2;
?>
```

> **Note: Please Note that in PHP, we need not to tell PHP that variable is of which data type like in other languages as PHP accordingly converts and assigns the variable to the correct data type depending on the value of variable.**

CHAPTER 3

Operators and Control Statements

3.1 Introduction

Operators are the inputs to PHP processor to perform certain actions related to logical and mathematical operations. The work of operators is similar like in other programming languages i.e. Programming in C. In Table 3.1, we have discussed the operators used in PHP.

Table 3.1: Operators in PHP

Arithmetic Operators	Addition (+)	Subtraction (-)	Division (/)	Modulus (%)	Exponentiation (**)
Assignment Operator	x=y	x-=y means x=x-y	x/=y means x=x/y	x%=y means x=x%y	x**=y means x=x**y
Comparison	==(Equal)	!= Not equal or <> or !==	<(Less Than)	> =(Greater Than or equal to)	<=(Less Than or Equal to)
Increment/ Decrement Operators	++$i (Pre-increment) Increments $i by one, then returns $i	$i++(Post-Increment) Returns $i, then increments $i by one	$i—(Post-decrement) Returns $i, then decrements $i by one		
Logical Operators	AND (&&) Here output will be true if both $i && $j are true	OR(||) Here output will be true if both $i || $j are true	NOT (!) Here output is true if $i is not true i.e. (!$i)		
Assignment Operators	.(DOT) This operator is used for concatenation i.e. $i.$j	.= This operator in strings is used to append data of one variable to another i.e. $x.=$y, Here $y value will be combined together with $x.			

3.2 Control Statements

Control statements control the flow of execution of a program and allow to branch the execution of scripts based on the input and handle repetitive tasks using iterations.

> Here are two type of control structures in PHP: **Conditional Statements and Loops**

The following control statements along with examples are mentioned below:

Example 3.1: Using if, else-if, else conditions:

```
<html>
<body>
<?php
```

/* Here using Date Function, it will fetch the current day according to the built-in clock of the web server on which the PHP script executed. In this function if we pass "D" then it will return the textual representation of a day like Mon,Tue,Wed, etc. and if we pass "d" then it will return day of month in numeric form i.e. 01 to 31. */

```
$d=date("D");
if ($d=="Wed")
  echo "It is Wednesday!";
elseif ($d=="Mon")
  echo "It isMonday!";
else
  echo "Have a nice day!";
?>
</body>
</html>
```

Example 3.2

```
<?php
$i=10
$j=9
if($i>$j)
{
echo "i is greater than j";
}
elseif($i==$j)
{
echo "i is equal to j";
}
else
{
echo "i is less than j";
}
?>
```

Example 3.3: Use of Switch Statement

```
<?php
$course ="php";
switch($course)
{
```

```
case "php":
echo "You have chosen php as the subject";
break;
case "java":
echo "You have chosen java as the subject";
break;
case "C":
echo "You have chosen C as the subject";
break;
default:
echo "Your interest is towards another technology";
}
?>
```

The switch statement executes the statements line by line. In switch statement when a case statement is found, the expression is evaluated to a value which matches the value of the switch expression and PHP execute the statements. PHP continues to execute the statements until the end of the switch block, or when it sees the break statement.

> **Note: If you don't write a break statement at the end of a case's statement list, PHP will go on executing the statements of the following case. Please go through the examples mentioned below to see the difference of switch statement with break and without break statement.**

Example 3.4: Example of Switch Statement with Break and without Break

```
<?php
switch($i)
{
case 0:
echo "i value is equal to 0";
case 1:
echo "i value is equal to 1";
case 2:
echo "i value is equal to 2";
}
?>
<?php
switch($i)
{
case 0:
echo "i value is equal to 0";
break;
case 1:
echo "i value is equal to 1";
break;
case 2:
echo "i value is equal to 2";
break;
default:
echo "i value is neither equal to 0,1,2";
}
?>
```

3.3 Loops
While and Do while Loop

While and Do while loop both perform iterations but there is one basic difference in both loops that is in while loop condition gets evaluated on entry level and program will not execute until condition satisfies whereas in Do while loop, program runs at least once even if the condition not satisfies because in do while loop, the condition is not evaluated until the end of each loop.

To get more understanding of the difference between both loops, go through the examples mentioned below:

Example 3.5: While and Do while Loops

```php
<?php
$i = 1;
//here condition will be
checked at the entry
//leveland program will
not run if condition //is
false
while($i<=5)
{
echo     "The     Number
displayed is:$i<br>";
$i++;
}
?>
```

```php
<?php
$i = 1;
//here condition will
not be checked at the
//entry level and
program will run atleast
//once and then condi-
tion will be checked
do
{
echo     "The     Number
displayed is:$i<br>";
$i++;
} while($i<=5);
?>
```

Example 3.6: For Loop Statement

In for loop, three parameters are passed i.e. first statement is initial state, condition and finally increment or decrement statement.

```html
<html>
<head>
<title>For Loop</title>
</head>

<body>
<?php

for ($i = 0; $i <= 25; $i++) {
echo "the counter is: " . $i . "<br/>";
}
?>
```

```
</body>
</html>
```

Example 3.7 Another Example of For Loop

```php
<?php
for($i=12;$i<24;$i+=2)
{
echo $i."<br>";
}
?>
```

Note: In Example 3.7 variable 'i' value starts from 12, then condition is checked until we reach 24 and then value is incremented by 2. Here $i+=2 means $i =$i + 2.

CHAPTER 4

Arrays

4.1 What are Arrays?

An array is a data structure that contains group of elements having homogeneous data type. It is a special variable which can hold more than one value at a time.

In PHP, the array () function is used to create an array. In PHP, there are three types of arrays:

1. **Indexed Arrays:** Arrays with numeric index are called Indexed Arrays.
2. **Associative arrays:** These are the arrays with named keys.
3. **Multidimensional arrays:** It contains one or more arrays.

Example 4.1: Indexed Arrays

```
<? php
$course[0]="Php";
$course[1]="Asp.Net";
$course[2]="C#";
echo $course[0] . " and " . $course[1] . " are short term courses.";
?>
```

Example 4.2 Numeric Arrays using foreach () loop

The foreach loop works only with arrays. Here, it loops over arrays through each key/value pair in an array. In Example 4.2, for each loop over the array given by $number and on each iteration, the value of the current element i.e. $number [0] = 1, the next is $number [1] = 2 is assigned to $value and the internal array pointer is incremented by one so that on the next iteration, next element will be fetched.

```
<html>
<body>
<?php
/* First method to create array. */
$numbers = array (1, 2, 3, 4, 5);
foreach( $numbers as $value )
{
  echo "Value is $value <br />";
}
/* Second method to create array. */
$numbers[0] = "one";
$numbers[1] = "two";
$numbers[2] = "three";
$numbers[3] = "four";
$numbers[4] = "five";
```

```php
foreach( $numbers as $value )
{
  echo "Value is $value <br />";
}
?>
</body>
</html>
```

Example 4.3

In this example, **asort() function** is used to do sorting.

```php
<html>
<head>
<title>foreach and associative arrays</title>
</head>
<body bgcolor="#f9f9f9">
<?php
$course = array( "Java"=>"6 weeks", "php"=>"4 weeks") ;
<h3>Courses Duration are</h3>
asort($course);
print "<p>" ;
foreach($course as $a => $b)
{
print "The duration of $a is $b </p>" ;
}
print "</p>" ;
?>
</p>
</form>
</body>
</html>
```

4.2 Associative Arrays

The associative arrays are very similar to numeric arrays in term of functionality but they are different in terms of their index. Associative array will have their index as string so that you can establish a strong association between key and values.

Example 4.4. Associative Arrays

```php
<html>
<body>
<?php

/* First method to create array. */
$fees = array(
```

```
            "java" => 7000,
            "c#" => 6000, /* Key-Value Pair */
            "asp" => 5000
            );
echo "Fees of Java is ". $fees['java'] . "<br />";
echo "Fees of C# is ".  $fees['c#']. "<br />";
echo "Fees of Asp is ".  $fees['asp']. "<br />";

/* Second method to create array. */

$fees['java'] = "high";
$fees['c#'] = "medium";
$fees['asp'] = "low";

echo "Fees of Java is ". $fees['java'] . "<br />";
echo "Fees of C# is ".  $fees['c#']. "<br />";
echo "Fees of Asp is ".  $fees['asp']. "<br />";
?>
</body>
</html>
```

Note: Don't keep associative array inside double quotes while printing otherwise it would not return any value.

4.3 Array Functions

There are many inbuilt array functions but we have discussed some examples of inbuilt array functions.

1.count () function used in Arrays:

To get the length of an array, we use count () function. The count () function is used to return the length (the number of elements) of an array.

Example 4.5. count () function in arrays:

```
<?php

$a=array ("php","asp","java");

echo count ($a);

?>
```

2.in_array () function:

in_array()function checks if a value exists in an array. The in_array () function search an array for a specific value.

Example 4.6 in_array () function in arrays:

```
<html>
<head>
<title>in_array</title>
</head>
<body>

<?php
$a = array ("Amit","Sunil");
if (in_array("amit",$a))
                    {
 echo "Amit is Found in Records";
                    }
                    else
                    {
                    echo "Amit is not found in Records";
                    }
        ?>
</body>
</html>
```

Note: If the search argument in array is a string type, then search is case-sensitive.

How to unset Arrays?

The unset() function destroys a given variable.

Example 4.7 Example of unset () function

```
<?php
// Create a simple array.
$array = array(1,2,3,4,5);
print "\n";
print_r($array); /* This function is used to print the array readable format */
// Now delete every item, but leave the array itself intact:
 foreach ($array as $i => $value)
 {
    unset($array[$i]);
 print "\n";
```

```
}

print_r($array);
?>
```

Example 4.8 Example of unset () function

```php
<?php
$a = array(14,26,13,55,15);
unset($a[2]);
print_r($a);
```

Output:

```
Array
(
    [0] => 14
    [1] => 26
    [3] =>55
    [4] =>15
)
```

4.4 Multidimensional Arrays

In multi-dimensional array each element in the main array can also be an array, and each element in the sub-array can be an array, and so on. Values in the multi-dimensional array are accessed by using multiple indexes.

Example 4.9. Multi-Dimensional Array

```php
<html>
<body>
<?php
  $marks = array(
                  "A" => array
                  (
                  "PHP" => 35,
                  "ASP" => 30,
                  "C++" => 39
                  ),
                  "B" => array
          (
          "PHP" => 30,
          "ASP" => 32,
          "C++" => 29
```

```
        ),
        "C" => array
        (
        "A" => 31,
        "B" => 22,
        "C" => 39
        )
        );
/* Accessing multi-dimensional array values */
  echo "Marks for A in PHP : " ;
  echo $marks['A']['PHP'] . "<br />";
  echo "Marks for B in ASP : ";
  echo $marks['B']['ASP'] . "<br />";
  echo "Marks for C in C++ : " ;
  echo $marks['C']['C++'] . "<br />";
?>
</body>
</html>
```

CHAPTER 5

Functions

5.1 What are Functions?

A function is a set of statements which can be used multiple times in a program as per the need.

A function can be reused and it saves the memory space and time.

A function will not execute itself, it will work only when it is called to perform some function.

A function takes input in the form of parameters, does processing and returns some value.

There are two type of functions, one is in-built functions where the set of statements are already written in system and other is user defined where the function is written by the user itself. Here we have discussed the examples of user defined functions.

Example 5.1 Function

```
<html>
<head>
<title>Function Simplest Example</title>
</head>

<body>
<?php

/* Called Function */

function MyFunction()  /* Here the function "MyFunction"  is defined   but it will not
execute until it is not called */
{
echo "This is being displayed because MyFunction has been called" ;
}

/* Calling Function */

MyFunction();/*  Here the Function is called and now it will execute after reading this
function */
?>
</body>
</html>
```

Example 5.2 Functions using Parameters

```
<html>
<head>
<title>Parameterized Function</title>
</head>

<body>
<?php

/* function MyList is defined and three parameters are taken */

function MyList ($first, $second, $third)
{
echo "Firstname is: " . $first . "<br/> ";
echo "Secondname is: " . $second . "<br/> ";
echo "Thirdname is:" . $third . "<br/>";
}
/* Here another Function with the name AddThese, is defined and again three
parameters are taken */

function AddThese($first, $second, $third)

$answer = $first + $second + $third ;
return $answer ; /* Here integervalue is returned*/
}



MyList ("Akshit", "Sunil", "Suresh"); /* Here Function is called and Parameters are
                                        passed in function*/
```

```php
echo "<br/><br/>";

$first = 5 ;
$second = 34 ;
$third = 237 ;

$math = AddThese($first, $second, $third);

echo "$first, $second, and $third add up to: " . $math;
?>
</body>
</html>
```

5.2 Call by value and Call by reference

In call by value the value is passed directly to a function where it is defined or called function and if the called function uses the values in some variable and make any changes to it, even then it will not affect the source variable or actual variable where-as in call by reference, the address of a variable is passed rather than the value and if any changes made in called function, then it will surely affect the actual variable because passing address of a variable means where the actual value is stored.

To better understand the difference, please go through the below mentioned example.

Example 5.3 Call by value and Call by reference

```php
<html>
<head>
<title>Call by value</title>
</head>
<body>
<?php
function displayit($text)
{
echo $text ;
}
$message = "say hello to the php world";
displayit($message) ;
?>
</body>
</html>
```

```php
<html>
<head>
<title>Call by reference</title> </head>
<body>
<?php
/*Here address & variable is used */
function displayit(&$text)
{
        $text.="to the php world";
}
$message="say hello";
displayit($message);
echo $message;
?>
</body>
</html>
```

Note: Function Names are not case-sensitive.

5.3 PHP Include and Require Statements

In PHP, include () and require () statements are predefined functions to insert the content of one PHP file to another PHP file before the server executes the program. Both, include and require statements are very helpful when there is need to insert module program in another file to be used multiple times to run the script. For example in case of databases the configuration file containing database configuration is used multiple times for running the database programs.

Both include and require statements perform the same work but there is one basic difference between both statements.

In include statement, if there is any problem in loading a file then include() function generates a warning but the script will continue execution whereas In require statement, if there is any problem in loading a file then require () function generates a fatal error and halt the execution of the script.

Please go through the example mentioned below for better understanding of include and require statements:

Example 5.4
1. In order to run the example, first save the files as mentioned in Example.

check.php

```php
<?php
$course='PHP';
$institute='NIELIT';
?>
```

statement.php

```
<html>
<body>

<h1>Welcome to my home page</h1>
```

/* Here the two variables $course and $institute are declared in check.php file and we are using it in 'statement.php' file because we have included the file here. */

```php
<?php include 'check.php';
echo "I have done $course from $institute";
```

```
?>

</body>
</html>
```

Note: In require () statement, if the file check.php is missing, then execution of the script will halt and it will generates a fatal error whereas in include, the script will run with warning message.

CHAPTER 6

Strings

6.1 Introduction

A string is a sequence of characters like "PratiyushGuleria". In this chapter, we have discussed some commonly used inbuilt functions of strings.

Example 6.1 String Concatenation

```
<html>
<head>
<title>Strings</title>
</head>
<?php
$a="Raj";
$b="Kumar";
?>
<?php
$c=$a;
$c.=$b; /*String Concatenation using . operator */ $d="working in IT Industry";
$c.=$d;
echo $c;
?>
<body>
</body>
</html>
```

Example 6.2 In-Built Functions of Strings

```
<html>
<head>
<title>Predefined String Functions</title>
</head>
<body>
<?php
$iststring="anil KUMAR kamal pankaj";?>
/* Here strtolower() function lowercase the characters */ lowercase:-<?php echo
strtolower($iststring);?><br/>
/* Here strtoupper() function uppercase the characters */ Uppercase:-<?php echo
strtoupper($iststring);?><br/>
```

```
/* ucfirst() function uppercase the First Character */
Upper case First character:-<?php echo ucfirst($iststring);?><br/>

/* ucwords() function is used to uppercase the words */
uppercase word:-<?php echo ucwords($iststring);?><br/>

/* strlen() function to find out the length of the string */
length of string:- <?php echo strlen($iststring);?><br/>

/* trim() function used to trim the left and right spaces of string */
trim:-<?php echo trim($iststring);?><br/>

/* strstr() function is used to locate and search for the first occurrence of a
string inside another string */
find:-<?php echo strstr($iststring,"kamal");?><br/>

/* str_replace() function is used to replace the string with another string */
replace:-<?php echo str_replace("anil","abc",$iststring);?><br/>

/* str_repeat() is the function to repeat a string */
repeat:--<?php echo str_repeat($iststring,50);?><br/>

/* substr() function is used to find out some part of the string in a given string
providing some specified location */

make sub string:-<?php echo substr($iststring,35,64);?><br/>

/* strops() function is used to find out the position of the string */

find position:-<?php echo strpos($iststring,"kamal");?><br/>

/* The strchr() function searches for the first occurrence of a string inside
another string */

length of character:-<?php echo strchr($iststring,"P");?><br/>

</body>
</html>
```

Example 6.3 strstr () function example

```
<? php
$email = 'pratiyushguleria@gmail.com';
$domain = strstr($email, '@');
echo $domain;
$user = strstr($email, '@', true);
```

```
echo $user;
if($domain ==".com")
{
echo "email address is valid";
}
else
{
echo "email address is not valid";
}
?>
```

CHAPTER 7

Form Processing

7.1 Introduction

Form Processing is essential part of PHP where data submitted by using HTML forms is processed by PHP which makes the normal static page of HTML to Dynamic Page. There are two important methods i.e. GET and POST in PHP, by using which information submitted in HTML form is processed by PHP.

There are two important attributes which are to be submitted in HTML static page is HTML form element's method attribute and another is to specify the location of the PHP file that will process the information.

7.2 $_GET and $_POST

$_GET and $_POST are the PHP superglobal variables i.e. predefined global variables which are used to collect form-data and as global word means that they are always accessible from any function, class or file regardless of their scope.

These both GET and POST create an array in the form of Key/Value pair where keys are the names of the form controls and values are the input data from the user. E.g. array (key => value, key2 => value2, key3 => value3).

When to use GET?

$_GET method used in HTML form, an array of variables is passed to the current script via URL parameters.

Information sent from a form with the GET method is visible to everyone (all variable names and values are displayed in the URL).

$_GET also has limits on the amount of information to send. However, because the variables are displayed in the URL, it is possible to bookmark the page. This can be useful in some cases.

GET may be used for sending non-sensitive data.

Note: GET should never be used for sending passwords or other sensitive information!

Wthen to use POST?

$_POST is an array of variables which is passed to the current script via the HTTP POST method.

Information sent from a form with the POST method is invisible to others (all names/values are embedded within the body of the HTTP request)

Has no limit on the amount of information to send. Moreover POST supports advanced functionality such as support for multi-part binary input while upload-ing files to server. However, because the variables are not displayed in the URL, it is not possible to bookmark the page.

$_POST method is more secure as compare to $_GET method.

Example 7.1 Form Processing:
In order to run the program, please save the files as mentioned below:

1. Save the HTML program with filename "login.php"
2. Create new page with filename "next.php"

Login.php

```
<html>
<head>
<title>Log-In Page</title>
</head>
<body>
 Please enter your user details to log-in here...
<form action = "next.php" method = "POST">
Username :<br>
<input type = "text" name = "user">          First Parameter
<br><br>
 Password:<br>
<input type = "password" name = "pass">       Second Parameter
<br><br>
<input type = "submit" value = "Log In" name="submit">
</form>
</body>
</html>
```

next.php

```
<?php                           First Parameter is passed here
$username = $_POST ["user"];
$password = $_POST ["pass"];     Second Parameter is passed here
echo "Your username and password is". $username."". $password;
?>
```

Example 7.2 Form Processing Example using Checkboxes, Radio Buttons:
In order to run the program, please save the files as mentioned below:

1. Save the HTML program with filename "test.php".
2. Create new page with filename "process.php".

test.php

```html
<html>
<head>
 <title>Process the HTML form data with the POST method</title>
</head>
<body>
 <form name="myform" action="process.php" method="POST">

  Name: <input type="text" name="fname" /><br />
  FatherName: <input type="text" name="fathername" maxlength="10" /><br />
  Select course from the list:
<select name="course">
   <option value="C" selected="selected">C</option>
   <option value="ASP">ASP</option>
   <option value="JAVA">JAVA</option>
   <option value="ANDROID">ANDROID</option>
  </select><br /><br />
  Choose the Training Type:
 <input type="radio" name="Training" value="ShortTerm" />Short Term
 <input type="radio" name="Training" value="LongTerm" />Long Term
  <input type="radio" name="Training" value="Industrial"/> Industrial
  <br />
  Choose the course duration:
       <input type="checkbox" name="Duration[]" value="4weeks" checked="-
checked" /> Four Weeks
   <input type="checkbox" name="Duration[]" value="6weeks" /> Six Weeks
   <input type="checkbox" name="Duration[]" value="8weeks" /> Eight Weeks
   <input type="checkbox" name="Duration[]" value="6Months" /> Six Months
  <br /><br />
  Correspondence Address:<br />
   <textarea name="Address" rows="10" cols="60">Enter your Correspondence
Address here</textarea><br />
  <input type="submit" />
 </form>
</body>
</head>
</html>
```

Note: The Bold Letters in Example 7.2 are parameters

process.php

```php
<?php
  echo "Your name is: {$_POST['fname']}<br />";
  echo "Your fathername is: {$_POST['fathername']}<br />";
```

```
  echo "Course selected is: {$_POST['course']}<br /><br />";
  echo "Training choosen is: {$_POST['Training']}<br /><br />";

echo "Your correspondence address is:<br />{$_POST['Address']}<br /><br />";
  foreach($_POST['Duration'] as $duration)
{   echo "Duration of course is: {$duration}<br />";
}
?>
```

Example 7.3

```
<html>
<head>
</head>
<title>
Form Processing
</title>
<body>
<form action="array.php" method="POST">
<input type="checkbox" name="check_list[]" alt="Checkbox" value="C#">C#
<input type="checkbox" name="check_list[]" alt="Checkbox" value="VB">VB
<input type="checkbox" name="check_list[]" alt="Checkbox" value="PHP">PHP
<button type="submit">submit</button>
</form>
</body>
</html>
```

array.php

```
<?php

echo "Select The Course<pre>" ;
print_r($check_list) /*Display the Array Structure in Human Readable Form*/

echo "</pre>";
if(!empty($_POST['check_list']))
{
foreach($_POST['check_list'] as $check) /* it loops over arrays through each key/value
pair in an array  */
{
echo "Course you have selected is=$check<br>";
}
}
?>
```

Notice that there are square brackets [] used with the name of the checkbox element. The reason for the square brackets is that it informs PHP that the value may be an array of information. Users can select multiple values, and PHP will place them all into an array of the value of the name attribute.

Example 7.4 Email validation using Form Processing and strstr() function
File Name: "test.php"

```
<html>
<head>
</head>
<title>
Email Validation
</title>
<form action = "email.php" method = "post">
<body>
Enter Your email id  <input type = "text" name = "email">
<br/>
<input type = "submit" name = "submit">
</body>
</html>
```

"email.php":

strstr() **function** is used to locate and search for the first occurrence of a string inside another string.

```
<?php
$string1=$_POST["email"];
$newstring=strstr($string1,".com");
echo $newstring;
if($newstring==".com")
{
echo "email is valid";
}
else
{
echo "email is not valid";
}

?>
```

CHAPTER 8

Cookies And Sessions

8.1 Introduction

A cookie is a temporary file stored on client side and is used to identify a user. These files are embedded by the server on the client's computer and when the same computer requests a page with a browser, it will send the cookie too.

8.2 How to Create a Cookie?

The setcookie () function is used to set a cookie.

Note The setcookie () function must appear BEFORE the <html> tag

Example 8.1 Set a Cookie

```
<html>
<head>
<title>Cookies</title>
</head>

<body>

<!--A cookie is merely a small file that the web server stores on the hard drive of the client's machine. Cookies have names (to identify them) and values. They can also have expiry, location, and security settings, but these settings are optional. The following code defines two cookies in PHP: -->

$data = "this will be placed in the cookie";
setcookie("CookieName", $data) ;
setcookie("AnotherCookieName", $data, time()+60*60*24*30) ;

</body>
</html>
```

Example 8.2

```
<?php
setcookie("username", "Pratiyush", time()+60*60*24*30);
?>
```
In the example cookie is set with "username" and value is "Pratiyush" and in third parameter it sets the time after which cookie will expire.

8.3 How to Retrieve a Cookie Value?

The PHP $_COOKIE variable is used to retrieve a cookie value.

In the example below, we retrieve the value of the cookie named "username" and display it on a page:

Example 8.3 Retrieve Cookie Value
```php
<?php
// Print a cookie using variable which is set in Example 8.2
echo $_COOKIE["username"];

// A way to view all cookies
print_r($_COOKIE);
?>
```

In the following example the isset() function is used to find out if a cookie has been set in the previous examples or not:

Example 8.4 isset function used in cookies


```php
<html>
<body>

<?php
if (isset($_COOKIE["username"]))
  echo "Welcome " . $_COOKIE ["username"] . "!<br>";
else
  echo "Welcome guest!<br>";
?>

</body>
</html>
```

Example 8.5   Example of Cookies for Form Processing:

Please go through the example mentioned below for setting cookies by using Form Processing.
> **First file is saved with name "sample.html"**
> **Another file is "login.php"**

Sample.html
```html
<html>
<head>
<title>Set cookie and use in Form Processing</title>
```

```
</head>
<body>
<h2>User Login</h2>
<form name="login" method="POST" action="login.php">
  Username: <input type="text" name="username"><br>
  Password: <input type="password" name="password"><br>
<input type="submit" name="submit" value="Login!">
</form>
</body>
</html>
```

login.php

```php
<?php
$user = 'pratiyush';
$pass = 'guleria';

if (($_POST['username'] == $user) && ($_POST['password'] == $pass))
{
 setcookie('username', $_POST['username'], time()+60*60*24*365);
header('Location: check.php');  /* This statement will redirect the browser window to
the given location on execution*/
  }
    else
{
    echo 'Username/Password Invalid';
  }
?>
```

check.php:
```php
<?php

if (isset ($_COOKIE['username']))
{
  echo 'Welcome' . $_COOKIE ['username'];
 }
?>
```

8.4 Sessions

Sessions are stored on server side. A PHP session variable is used to store information about, or change settings for a user session. Session variables hold information about one single user, and are available to all pages in one application. For Example: In email, first we login with username and password, our session among the pages in email account will remain until we click on logout to destroy the complete session.

A session is started with the session_start () function. $_SESSION is a PHP global variable to set the session variable.

Example 8.6   Sessions

```php
<?php
/* to store and retrieve session variables is to use the PHP $_SESSION variable */
session_start();
$_SESSION['name'] = "pratiyush";
?>
/*   To Unset the Session   */
<?php
session_start();
unset($_SESSION['name']);

/* To Destroy the Session */
session_destroy();
?>
```

Example 8.7 Sessions Example with multiple pages

```php
/* page1.php  */
<?php
session_start();

echo 'Welcome in Institute ';

$_SESSION['course'] = 'DotNet';
$_SESSION['duration'] = 'sixweeks';


echo '<br /> <a href="next.php">Click for next page</a>';

?>

/* next.php */
<?php

session_start();

echo 'This is next page<br />';

echo $_SESSION['course']; /* Here the session id used in previous page will be used */
echo $_SESSION['duration'];
```

```
echo '<br /> <a href="page1.php">Click to go back in page 1</a>';
?>
```

Example 8.8 Sessions

"login.php"

```
<html>
<head>
<title>Login </title>
</head>
<body>
<?php
if (isset($_GET['error']))
{
$error=$_GET['error'];

if ($error==1)
{
echo "<font color='blue' size=4 name='arial'>";
echo "<center><h2> Login </h2></center><br/></font>";
echo "<font color='red' size=5 name='arial'>";
echo "<center><b> Username or Password Invalid Please Try Again
</center><br/><b></font>";
?>
<?php
}
}
?>
<center>
<table border="2">
<tr>
<td align="center">
<form name="frm" method="POST" action="check.php">
<center>Username: <input type="text" name="name"/>
Password: <input type="password" name="pwd"/></center>
<br/>
<input type="submit" value="Login" name="loginBtn"/>
</td>
</tr>
</table>
</center>
</body>
</html>
```

"check.php"

```php
<?php
if (isset($_POST['loginBtn']))
{
$user=trim($_POST['name']);
$pass=$_POST['pwd'];
if ($user=="admin"&&$pass=="admin")
{
session_start();
$_SESSION['user']=$_POST['name'];
$_SESSION['first_name']="Pratiyush";
$_SESSION['last_name']="Guleria";
header("location:home.php");
}
else if ($user=="123"&&$pass=="123")
{
session_start();
$_SESSION['user']=$_POST['name'];
$_SESSION['first_name']="NIELIT";
$_SESSION['last_name']="Pratiyush";
header("location:home.php");
}
else
{

/* Here "login.php" window will open if username and password mismatch.The
"error=1" is a flag to display message */
header("location:login.php?error=1");
}
}

?>
```

"home.php"

```php
<?php
session_start();
if (isset($_SESSION['user']))
{
?>

<?php
echo "<br><br>";
echo "<font color='blue' size=4>";
echo "Welcome ";
```

```php
echo $_SESSION['first_name'] .  " " . $_SESSION['last_name']."."; 
echo "</font>";
?>
<br><br>
<a href="logout.php" title="Click here to logout in the system">
<b>Logout</b></a>
<?php
}
else
{
header("location:login.php?error=1");
}

?>
```

"logout.php"

```php
<?php
session_start();
session_destroy();
header("location:login.php");
?>
```

CHAPTER 9

Databases

9.1 Introduction

MySQL is the popular database system used with PHP. In PHP, there are two ways to connect to database either by using MySQL console or phpmyAdmin.

Here Fig. 9.1 displays the MySQL Console where some commonly used SQL queries are executed. MySQL console will ask for the password for username "root" on opening the screen and at that moment, press enter key as password is not set and is blank.

Fig.9.2, displays another method to connect to database and for that in widget on taskbar, click on phpmyAdmin. It will open the Graphical User Interface for database administration in PHP.

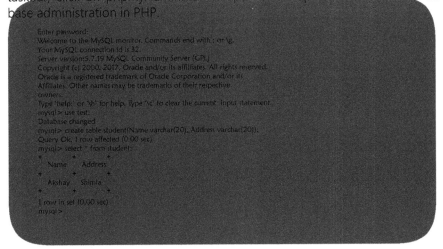

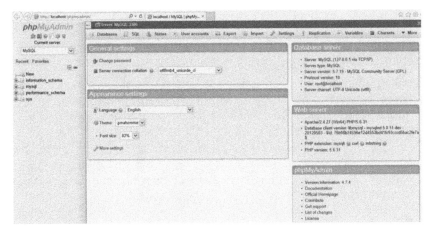

Fig.9.2: phpmyAdmin Graphical User Interface for Database Administration in PHP

> Note We can also import and export the database files using phpmyAdmin GUI Environment which are helpful for taking backup and restore data.

Example 9.1 Database Program to insert record

To run the program, first create the two attributes i.e. Name, Address and select the data type as varchar with size 20 in MySQL console or PhpmyAdmin GUI interface.

The database name used in this program is "php" and tablenameis "student".

database.html

```
<html>
<head>
</head>
<title>
</title>
<body>
<form method = "POST" action = "insertdatabase.php">

Enter The Name<input type = "text" name = "Name">
<br>
Enter The Address<input type ="text" name = "Address">
<br>
<input type = "submit" name = "click here">
<br>
</form>

</body>

</html>
```

insertdatabase.php

mysql_connect () function is used to open a database connection. It takes three parameters i.e. first parameter is hostname which is the server name **(usually "localhost"),** the second parameter is username that we have mentioned "root" and the third parameter is password which is mentioned blank "".

If there will be any exception in database connection, then using mysql_error() function, the exception statement will be displayed.

mysql_select_db () function sets the current active database on the server associated with connection established. Here, the current active database name is **"php"** and the second parameter consists of connection variable

$con.

Then SQL query to insert record into database is written. After execution of SQL statement, if any exception occurs to establish database connection or error in SQL query, then mysql_error () function shows the same else the record will be added into database successfully.

```php
<?php
error_reporting(0);
$con = mysql_connect ("localhost","root","");
if (!$con)
  {
  die('Could not connect:' .mysql_error());
  }

mysql_select_db ("php", $con);

$sql="INSERT INTO student (Name, Address) VALUES('$_POST[Name]','$_POST[Ad-
dress]')";

if (!mysql_query($sql,$con))
  {
  die('Error: ' . mysql_error());
  }
echo "1 record added";

mysql_close($con)
?>
```

Example 9.2 Database Program to display records inserted in Example 9.1

In this program, all the configurations remain same; we have just changed the SQL query.
mysql_fetch_array () function is used in the program to fetch the results from the database in the form of associative array, a numeric array or both. This function will return an array that corresponds to the fetched row and moves the pointer to the next row of the result.

```php
<?php
error_reporting(0);

$con = mysql_connect ("localhost","root","");
if(!$con)
{
die('could not connect:' .mysql_error());
```

```
}
mysql_select_db("php",$con);
$result = mysql_query("SELECT * FROM student");/* This query will display all the
records saved in student table */

echo "<table border='1'>
<tr>
<th>Name</th>
<th>Address</th>
</tr>";

while($row= mysql_fetch_array($result))
{
echo "<tr>";
echo "<td>".$row['Name']."</td>";
echo "<td>".$row['Address']."</td>";
echo "</tr>";
}
echo "</table>";
mysql_close($con);
?>
```

Example 9.3 Program to display records in dropdown box from Database:

In order to run this program, please go through the following steps:

Create database with name **"test"** and tablename **"testable"**.

Create two fields in database: **"ID"**, **"Name"** and enter some values into the table.

mysql_numrows () function count the number of rows and it requires more than zero value in table. This function expects parameter 1 as Boolean value.

```
<?php
error_reporting(0);

$connection = mysql_connect("localhost","root","");
$db = mysql_select_db("test",$connection);

echo "<select name=\"category\">";

$results= mysql_query("SELECT ID, Name from testtable ",$connection);
$id = "ID";
$idname = "Name";
```

```
echo mysql_error();

if (mysql_numrows($results)>0)
{
  $numrows=mysql_numrows($results);
  $x=0;
  while ($x<$numrows)

  {
    $Idfield=mysql_result($results,$x,$id);
    $Namefield=mysql_result($results,$x,$idname);
    echo "<option value=\"$Idfield\">$Namefield</option>\n";
    $x++;
  }
}
echo "</select>";
?>
```

Example 9.4 Program to search records in a Database:

To run this program, please go through the following instructions:
>   Create database with name **"bookstore"** and tablename **"books"**.

>   Create two fields in database: **"title varchar (30)", "author varchar (20)", "isbn number", "price number"** and enter some values into the table.

>   **htmlspecialchars () function** is used in the example as this function converts special characters to HTML entities. This function is used as one of the security measures as it prevent the web applications using forms from vulnerable attacks like Cross-site Scripting attacks i.e. attackers inject client-side script into Web Pages viewed by other users

"book.html"

```
<html>
<head>
<title>Catalog Search</title>
</head>
<body>
<h1></h1>
<form action="searchresults.php" method="post">
Choose Search Type:<br />
<select name="searchtype">/* FIRST PARAMETER */
<option value="author">Author</option>
<option value="title">Title</option>
```

```
<option value="isbn">ISBN</option>
</select>
<br />
Enter Search Term:<br />
<input name="searchterm" type="text" size="40"/>/* SECOND PARAMETER */
<br />
<input type="submit" name="submit" value="Search"/>
</form>
</body>
</html>
```

"searchresults.php"

```
<html>
<head>
<title></title>
</head>
<body>
<h1>Search Results</h1>
<?php
error_reporting(0);

$searchtype=$_POST['searchtype'];
```

/* Here trim function is used to remove any kind of spaces in the textbox */

```
$searchterm=trim($_POST['searchterm']);

if (!$searchtype || !$searchterm) {
echo 'You have not entered search details. Please go back and try again.';
exit;
}
```

/ * Here database connection and database is selected */

```
$con = mysql_connect("localhost","root","");
$db = mysql_select_db("bookstore", $con);
if (mysqli_connect_errno())
{
echo 'Error: Could not connect to database. Please try again later.';
exit;
}
```

/* Here select query is used to display all those books which matches with the "search-term" value passed in textbox. Here LIKE operator is used in a WHERE clause to

search for a specified pattern in a column and for that % sign is used which represents zero, one or multiple characters.   */

$query = "select * from books where ".$searchtype." like '%".$searchterm."%'";

$result=mysql_query($query);
$num_results=mysql_num_rows($result);

echo "<p>Number of books found: ".$num_results."</p>";
for ($i=0; $i <$num_results; $i++)
{

/* mysql_fetch_assoc () function is used to return an associative array that corresponds to the fetched row. This function is equivalent to mysql_fetch_array () function.   */

$row = mysql_fetch_assoc ($result);

echo "<p> ".($i+1).". Title: ";

/* stripslashes() function is used to remove backslashes added by the addslashes() function. The basic purpose of this function is to clean up the data retrieved from a database or from an HTML form.*/

echo htmlspecialchars(stripslashes($row['title']));
echo "
Author: ";
echo stripslashes($row['author']);
echo "
ISBN: ";
echo stripslashes($row['isbn']);
echo "
Price: ";
echo stripslashes($row['price']);
echo "</p>";
}

?>
</body>
</html>

Example 9.5 Program to delete records in a Database using Checkboxes:

Objective of Program: In this program email from databases will be fetched and we can delete the email from the database by using checkboxes. The output window of the program is shown in Figure 9.3.

To run this program, please go through the following instructions:

Fig.9.3: Delete Records using Checkboxes

Create database with name **"checkbox"** and tablename **"email1"**.

Create two fields in database: **"id number"**, **"firstname varchar (20)"**, **"lastname varchar (20)"**, **"email varchar (20)"** and enter some records into the table.

Here $_SERVER ['PHP_SELF'] in action attribute means that it will default to the current URL and it will submit the form to the same place it came from. The action will not be for another page; rather action will be submitted for the current page only i.e. the filename of the currently executing script.

Here for each loop is used which means that it loops over arrays through each key/value pair in an array where to delete [] array parameter which act as key is passed in checkboxes name attribute in form and $deleteid variable will act as storage for values assigned.

```
<html>
<head>

<title>Display and Remove Emails using Checkboxes</title>
<p>Please select the email addresses to delete from the email list and click Remove.
</p>

/* Here $_SERVER ['PHP_SELF'] in action attribute means that it will default
to the current URL and it will submit the form to the same place it came from.
The action will not be for another page; rather action will be submitted for the
current page only i.e. the filename of the currently executing script. */

<form method="post" action="<?php echo $_SERVER['PHP_SELF']; ?>">

<?php
error_reporting(0);

/* MySQLi is a class where "i" extension means MySQL Improved. */
/* Here Fourth Parameter is databasename i.e "checkbox" */
```

```php
$dbc = mysqli_connect('localhost', 'root', '', 'checkbox')
    or die('Error connecting to MySQL server.');

/* Delete the rows only if the form has been submitted and it will be checked by using
isset () function in arrays */

if (isset($_POST['submit'])) {
/* Here foreach loop is used which means that it loops over arrays through each
key/value pair in an array where todelete[] array parameter which act as key is passed
in checkboxes name attribute in form and $deleteid variable will act as storage for
values assigned */
    foreach ($_POST['todelete'] as $deleteid) {
        $query = "DELETE FROM email1 WHERE id = $deleteid";
        mysqli_query($dbc, $query)
            or die('Error querying database.');
    }

    echo 'Email of Person removed.<br />';
}

/* Display the rows with checkboxes for deleting */

$query = "SELECT * FROM email1";
$result = mysqli_query($dbc, $query);
while ($row = mysqli_fetch_array($result)) {
    echo '<input type="checkbox" value="' . $row['id'] . '" name="todelete[]" />';
    echo $row['firstname'];
    echo ' ' . $row['lastname'];
    echo ' ' . $row['email'];
    echo '<br />';
}

mysqli_close($dbc);
?>

<input type="submit" name="submit" value="Remove" />
</form>
</body>
</html>
```

Example 9.6 Example of TextArea and Databases:

To run this example, do the following steps:
Create the database "feedback" and tablename is "stufeed".

Here fieldname taken in table is "feedback".

"save.php"

$_REQUEST is a Superglobal variable and also known as HTTP Request variables.

It is an associative array which by default contains the contents of **$_GET, $_POST and $_COOKIE.**

```html
<html>
<body>
<form method="post" action="">
<textarea rows='10' cols='80' name='comments'>
</textarea>
<br>
<input type="submit" name="submit" value="Add Record"
title="Click here to add record in the database." size=50>
</form>
<?php
error_reporting(0);

$connect = mysql_connect("localhost","root","");
$select = mysql_select_db("feedback",$connect);
if ($_REQUEST['submit']){
        $comments = $_REQUEST['comments'];

        $qry = mysql_query("INSERT INTO stufeed SET feedback='$comments'");
        if ($qry){
                header("Location: read.php");
        }
}
?>
</body>
</html>
```

"read.php"

```html
<html>
<body bgcolor="lightgreen">
<style type="text/css">
textarea {
font-size: 1.5em;
}
</style>
<?php
```

```
error_reporting(0);

$connect = mysql_connect("localhost","root","");
$select = mysql_select_db("feedback",$connect);

$feedbackqry=mysql_query("select * from stufeed");
echo "<br>";
echo "<center><h2> Display Text in Text Area </h2></center>";
 echo "<br>";
echo "<center><textarea rows='20' cols='80' name='quote'> " ;
while($row = mysql_fetch_array($feedbackqry))
        {
        echo $row['comments'];
            }
             echo "</textarea></center>";
?>

</body>
</html>
```

9.2 Joins in SQL

Joins are used to combine rows from two or more tables and for fetching data based on a related column between them. In Joins SELECT Statement is used.

There are different types of SQL Joins:

1. INNER JOIN: It return records that have matching values in both tables.

2. LEFT JOIN: It will return all records from the left table and the matched records from the right table.

3. RIGHT JOIN: It will return all records from the right table and the records matched from the left table.

4. FULL JOIN: It will return all records when there is a match in either left or right table.

Example 9.7 Example of Inner Join:

Objective of Program: In this program records will be inserted into four different tables and records will be fetched on the basis of common id generated using **mysql_insert_id ()** function. Here, in SQL Query **inner join is used to fetch the records from multiple tables using the common id and return records that have matching values in all four tables.**

To run this program, please go through the following instructions:

Create database with name **"data"** and 4 tables along with their fields mentioned in table 9.1 below :

Table 9.1: Database Structure

Tablename	Location	Institute	User	Job
Fields Primary Key	Fieldname lid	Fieldname iid	Fieldname uid	Fieldname jid
	address	iname	name	job
				course

In this example, mysql_insert_id() function is used which returns the AUTO_INCREMENT ID generated from the previous INSERT operation. This function returns 0 if the previous operation does not generate an AUTO_INCREMENT ID, or FALSE on MySQLconnection failure.

"add.php"

```
<html>
<head>

<title>Add Record in Multiple Tables</title>
</head>

<body>

<form method="post" action="" name="form1" id="form1" >
<table width="533" border="0">
<tr>
<td width="64">Enter your Name</td>
<td width="459"><label>
<input type="text" name="name" size=65 />
</label></td>
</tr>
<tr>
<td>Course Interested For</td>
<td><input type="text" name="course" size=65 /></td>
</tr>
<tr>
<td>Institute</td>
<td><input type="text" name="institute" size=65 /></td>
```

```
</tr>
<tr>
<td>Address</td>
<td><input type="text" name="address" size=65 /></td>
</tr>
<tr>
<td>Job/Occupation</td>
<td><input type="text" name="job"  size=65/></td>
</tr>
</table>
<br>
<input type="submit" name="save" value="Save Record">
<a href="join.php"> View Records </a>
</form>
</body>
</html>

<?php

error_reporting(0);

if($_POST['save'])
{
 $connection = mysql_connect ("localhost", "root","")
  or die  (mysql_error());

 mysql_select_db ("data");/* Database Name is "data" */

  $name=$_POST['name'];
  $course=$_POST['course'];
  $institute=$_POST['institute'];
  $address=$_POST['address'];
  $job=$_POST['job'];
```

/* Here validation is performed to check whether the textboxes are blank and if blank, then message displayed that Textfield cannot be empty */

```
 if (empty($name) || empty($course)  ||
    empty($institute) || empty($address) ||
         empty($job))
 {
  echo " <br><center><h2> Textfield cannot be empty. </center></h2>";
  exit();
  }
        else {
```

```php
/* user table */

   $query_1="INSERT INTO user (uid, name, course) VALUES (NULL, '$name',
'$course')";
 mysql_query($query_1);

// Get the previous ID of the first query statement
// in order to connect the 3 remaining queries in the
// 3 different tables

$lastid=mysql_insert_id();

/*institute table */

$query_2="INSERT INTO institute (iid, iname) VALUES ($lastid, '$institute')";
 mysql_query($query_2);

/* location table */

$query_3="INSERT INTO location (lid, address) VALUES ($lastid, '$address')";
 mysql_query($query_3);

/*job table */

$query_4="INSERT INTO job (jid, job) VALUES ($lastid, '$job')";
 mysql_query($query_4);

 mysql_close($connection);

 echo "<br><br>";
 echo " <h3>Record has been save in the database </h3>";
 }
}
?>
```

join.php:

In join.php, SELECT query is used to fetch the records having common values in multiple tables using primary key.mysql_insert_id () function is used which returns the AUTO_INCREMENT ID in multiple tables.

In SELECT query, "AND" operator is used to check the logical conditions which means that all the conditions in query is to be true.

```php
<?php
error_reporting(0);
```

```
$dblocalhost = 'localhost';
$dbusername = 'root';
$dbpassword = '';
$conn = mysql_connect($dblocalhost, $dbusername, $dbpassword);
if(! $conn )
{
  die('Could not connect: ' . mysql_error());
}
$sql = 'SELECT user.name, user.course, institute.iname,
      location.address,job.job
      FROM user,institute,location,job
      WHERE user.uid = institute.iid
                AND user.uid = location.lid
                AND user.uid = job.jid';

mysql_select_db('data');
$result = mysql_query( $sql, $conn );
if(! $result )
{
  die('Could not get data: ' . mysql_error());
}
echo "<h3><center> USING INNER JOIN IN PHP/MySQL </h3></center>";


while($row = mysql_fetch_array($result, MYSQL_ASSOC))
{
   echo "Name : {$row['name']}    <br> ".
       "Course      : {$row['course']} <br> ".
       "Institute     : {$row['institute']} <br> ".
"Address      : {$row['address']} <br> ".
       "Occupation          : {$row['job']} <br> ".
       "================================<br>";
}
echo "<b> Fetched data successfully\n </b>";
mysql_close($conn);
?>
```

Example 9.8 Updating record in databases

Here record will be updated in the database using where clause with update commands. In where clause, id is checked in the database which is the primary key to update the record. The database structure is mentioned below:

Database Name = "data"

Table Name="student"
Attributes = stu_id int(10) PRIMARY KEY,stu_name varchar(30)

```php
<html>

<head>
<title>Update a Record in Database</title>
</head>

<body>
<?php
error_reporting(0);

    if(isset($_POST['update'])) {

      $con = mysql_connect("localhost", "root", "");

      if(! $con ) {
        die('Could not connect: ' . mysql_error());
      }

      $student_id = $_POST['stu_id'];
      $student_name = $_POST['stu_name'];

      $sql = "UPDATE student ". "SET stu_name = $student_name ".
        "WHERE stu_id = $student_id" ;
      mysql_select_db('data');
      $result = mysql_query( $sql, $con );

      if(! $result ) {
        die('Could not update data: ' . mysql_error());
      }
      echo "Updated data successfully\n";

      mysql_close($con);
    }else {
      ?>
<form method = "post" action = "<?php $_PHP_SELF ?>">
<table width = "400" border =" 0" cellspacing = "1"
          cellpadding = "2">

<tr>
<td width = "100">Student ID</td>
<td><input name = "stu_id" type = "text" id = "stu_id"></td>
```

```
</tr>

<tr>
<td width = "100">Student Name</td>
<td><input name = "stu_name" type = "text" id = "stu_name"></td>
</tr>

<tr>
<td width = "100"></td>
<td></td>
</tr>

<tr>
<td width = "100"></td>
<td>
<input name = "update" type = "submit" id = "update" value = "Update">
</td>
</tr>

</table>
</form>
<?php
    }
   ?>

</body>
</html>
```

CHAPTER 10

Validations and File Handling

10.1 Introduction

Form validation is done in order to check that a system meets the requirements and specifications as per the requirement set in the form and the intended purpose of validation is fulfilled.

10.2 Cascading Style Sheets

- ✓ CSS is used for describing the presentation of web pages layouts, colors, fonts etc.
- ✓ CSS saves a lot of work of design layouts of multiple web pages and handles the look and feel part of web pages.
- ✓ In Example **Cascading Style Sheet (CSS) is used where error class is** defined to highlight error if the values passed in the forms are not correct and requires validation.
- ✓ Regular Expressions are used to perform validation and for that preg_match () function is used which searches string for pattern, returning true if pattern exists, and false otherwise.

Example 10.1 Form validation using PHP

In order to run the program, please go through the following instructions:

- ✓ Create a separate file in notepad for cascading style sheet i.e. "style.css" and save this file in the same folder where the php file "validate.php" is saved.
- ✓ $_SERVER ["PHP_SELF"] variable is used in the example which sends the submitted form data to the page itself instead of moving to a different page. Here, the user will get error messages on the same page as the form but using this variable directly is prone to vulnerable attacks, therefore instead of using it directly, it must be used with htmlspecialchars() function. For Example : <form method="post" action="<?php echo htmlspecialchars($_ SERVER["PHP_SELF"]);?>">

"validate.php"

```
<html>
<head>
<title></title>
<link rel="stylesheet" type="text/css" href="style.css" />
</head>
<body>
```

```
<h3>Registration</h3>
<?php
 if (isset($_POST['submit'])) {
   $first_name = $_POST['firstname'];
     $email = $_POST['email'];
   $phone = $_POST['phone'];
     $flag = 'no';

   if (empty($first_name)) {
```

/* Here, error class is called from "style.css" file to display error in Red color if the form is not validated */

```
       echo '<p class="error">You forgot to enter your first name.</p>';
     $flag = 'yes';
    }


   if (!preg_match('/^[a-zA-Z0-9][a-zA-Z0-9\._\-&!?=#]*@/', $email)) {
       echo '<p class="error">Your email address is invalid.</p>';
     $flag = 'yes';
    }

   if (!preg_match('/^[0-9\/-]+$/', $phone)) {
     // $phone is not valid
     echo '<p class="error">Your phone number is invalid.</p>';
       $flag = 'yes';
    }

 }
 else {
   $flag = 'yes';
 }

 if ($flag == 'yes') {
?>
```

```
<form method="post" action="<?php echo htmlspecialchars($_SERVER["PHP_
SELF"]); ?>">
<p></p>
<table>
<tr>
<td>First Name:</td>
<td><input name="firstname" type="text"/></td></tr>

<tr>
<td>Email:</td>
<td><input name="email" type="text"/></td></tr>
<tr>
<td>Phone:</td>
<td><input name="phone" type="text"/></td></tr>

</table>

<input type="submit" name="submit" value="Submit" />
</p>
</form>

<?php
 }

?>
</body>
</html>
```

"style.css"

```
/* error class is defined in CSS */
.error {
 font-weight: bold;
 color: #FF0000;
}
```

10.3 File Handling Operations

File Handling is an important part of web applications and are used for storing data. In the example below, following file handling operations is performed i.e.

- ✓ Creating File
- ✓ Deleting File
- ✓ Reading File
- ✓ Writing File
- ✓ Appending File

Example 10.2 File Handling Operations

- ✓ In the following example, enctype (Encode Type) attribute is used which specifies the manner in which the form-data should be encoded when submitting it to the server.
- ✓ The multipart/form-data is one of the values of enctype attribute of form element. The multi-part attribute divides the form data into multiple parts and sends it to server.

```html
<html>
<head>
</head>
<title>
File Handling Operations
</title>

<form method="post" name="fileupload" enctype="multipart/form-data" action="">
<table border="1" cellpadding="2" cellspacing="2">
<tr>
<td>File Name</td>
<td><input type="text" name="file_name" id="file_name" /></td>
</tr>
<tr>
<td>File Content</td>
<td><input type="text" name="filedata" id="filedata" /></td>
</tr>
<tr>
<td> </td>
<td>
<input type="submit" name="createfile" id="createfile" value="Create"/>
```

```
<input type="submit" name="deletefile" id="deletefile" value="Delete"/>
<input type="submit" name="readfile" id="readfile" value="Read"/>
<input type="submit" name="writedata" id="writedata" value="Write"/>
<input type="submit" name="appendfile" id="appendfile" value="Append"/>
</td>
</tr>
</table>
</form>
```

/* Here createfile is passed as parameter and is checked using isset() function.In PHP touch is used to set access and modification time of file. */

```php
<?php
if(isset($_POST['createfile']))
{
  if(touch($_POST['file_name']))
  {
    echo 'File Created';
  }
  else
  {
    echo 'Some Problem';
  }

}
```

/* Here deletefile is passed as parameter and is checked using isset() function.In PHP unlink is used to delete the file. */

```php
if(isset($_POST['deletefile']))
{
  if(unlink($_POST['file_name']))
  {
    echo 'File Deleted';
  }
  else
  {
    echo 'Some Problem';
  }
```

```
}
/* fopen() is used to open the file and "w" is the mode for writing the data into
file */

if(isset($_POST['writedata']))
{
  $fp=fopen($_POST['file_name'],w);
  if(fwrite($fp,$_POST['filedata']))
  {
    echo 'Data Written into file';
  }
   else
   {
     echo 'Some Problem in file writing';
   }
}
```
/* fopen () is used to open the file and "r" is the mode for reading the data from the file. The fread () reads data from an open file. In this function, first parameter is passed as filename and the second parameter is passed as the number of bytes to be read from file. */

```
if(isset($_POST['readfile']))
{
  $fp=fopen($_POST['file_name'],r);
  echo fread($fp,100);
}
```
/* fopen () is used to open the file and "a" is the mode for appending the data from the file. The append() method insert the data at the end of the existing file.*/

```
if(isset($_POST['appendfile']))
{
  $fp=fopen($_POST['file_name'],a);
  if(fwrite($fp,$_POST['filedata']))
  {
    echo 'Data Appended in existing file';
  }
   else
   {
```

```php
   echo 'Some Problem occurred';
  }
}


?>
```

Example 10.3fwrite () in File Handling

- ✓ In the below mentioned example, fopen () function is used along with write "w" mode for writing data into file.
- ✓ The fwrite () function used in the example writes data to an open file.

```php
<?php
$myfile = "c:\welcome.txt";
$fp = fopen($myfile, 'w') or die("can't open file");
$stringData = "NIELIT\n";
fwrite($fp, $stringData);
$stringData = "Institute\n";
fwrite($fp, $stringData);
fclose($fh);
?>
```

Example 10.4 Reading character from file using loops

```php
<?php
$file=fopen("c:\data.txt","r") or exit("Unable to open file!");


/* Here the while loop will continue until the end of file(EOF) has been reached and for that the feof() function checks if the end of file has been reached */


while (!feof($file))
  {
  echo fgetc($file); /* fgetc() function is used to read the character from the file */
  }
fclose($file);
?>
```

CHAPTER 11

Object Oriented Programming

11.1 Introduction

PHP is object oriented scripting language and in this chapter we have covered some OOP concepts like classes, constructors, inheritance etc., through appropriate examples.

11.2 Classes and Objects

Class is a template or a structure consisting of variables and functions. In order to access them object of the class is defined by using new operator.

In Example $this variable is used. **$this is a special variable and is invoked when the method is called from within an object context. Here, $this is containing address of the calling object.**

Example 11.1. Example of Class

```php
<?php

/* The name of the class is "Myclass" */
class Myclass
{

/* $this variable is invoked in function or method containing the reference of the object $f */

public function display()
 {
 echo  $this->string_name;
 }
}
/* object is created using new operator */

$f = new MyClass;
$f->string_name = "NIELIT";
echo $f->display();
?>
```

In PHP, an object's properties can be set or accessed by using the following syntax (->):

Example 11.2. Example of Classes and objects accessing properties
"item.php"

```
/* Here variables are declared inside class structure */
<?php

class Item
{
public $itemID;
public $name;
public $price;
public $description;
}

?>
```

"Objectproperties.php"

Here using include statement class "item.php" is included

```
<?php
include 'item.php';

/* Here object of class "Item" is created */
$item1 = new Item();
$item1->itemID = '1001'; /* Set an objects property */

$item1->name = 'Book';
$item1->price = 200;
$item1->description= 'Programming Book';

$itemID = $item1->itemID; /* Access an objects property */
$name = $item1->name;
$price = $item1->price;
$description= $item1->description;

echo "Item ID is:" .$itemID ."<br/>";
echo "Name:" .$name."<br/>";
echo "Price is:".$price."<br/>";
echo "Description is".$description."<br/>";
?>
```

Note: $obj is an object that has already been instantiated.

Example 11.3 Example of Constructors:
11.3 Constructors

Special functions which are automatically called at moment an object is created.

Constructors never return values whereas functions return values.

Constructors are created by using __construct () function whereas in other programming languages constructor name is usually the class name.

A constructor allows initializing object properties.

```php
<?php
// Define a class
 class Myclass
 {
/*declaring three private variables. These private variables cannot be accessed directly. These
variables are used inside the display () method and this method is accessed by the object $f*/
 private $course;
 private $institute;
 private $fees;

/* Declare construct method which accepts three parameters   */

 function __construct($course,$institute,$fees)
 {
 $this->course = $course;
 $this->institute = $institute;
 $this->fees = $fees;
 }
/* Declare a display () method to display values */
 function display()
 {
 echo $this->course . "" . $this->institute."".$this->fees;
 }
 }

/* Create a  new object and pass three parameters */

 $f = new MyClass('Java','NIELIT','4000');

/* Call the method to display the string */

 echo $f->display();
 ?>
```

Here in __construct (), underscore is used twice.

Example 11.4. Example of Inheritance:
   • **extends keyword is used for inheritance**

```php
<?php
// Deflne a class
class Myclass
```

```php
{
/* protected modifier specifies that the member can only be accessed within its own
package. A protected member of a base class is accessible in a derived class only, if the
access occurs through the derived class type */
protected $location;
protected $course;
protected $institute;
// Declare construct method which accepts three parameters and the method display()
function __construct($location,$course,$institute)
{
$this->location = $location;
$this->course = $course;
$this->institute = $institute;
$this->display();
}
// Declare a method for display
public function display()
{
echo $this->location."".$this->course ."".$this->institute;
}
}

// Define a subclass "Mysubclass" inheriting properties of "Myclass" which is the base
class using extends keyword
class Mysubclass extends Myclass
{
// Call the method display().Here the variables declared in the Baseclass are inherited
in the subclass
public function display()
{
echo $this->location."".$this->course."".$this->institute;
}
}
// Create objects and passes parameters
$p = new Myclass('Shimla','Java','NIELIT');
$s = new Mysubclass('Shimla','.Net','DOEACC');
?>
```

CHAPTER 12

Regular Expressions and PDO Fundamentals

12.1 Introduction

Example 12.1Pattern Matching

preg_match() function is used to find pattern of regular expressions

In below mentioned example, program will echo "1" value. This is because, in program it will find one match for the regular expression.preg_match () will find the pattern "abc" in the larger string and if no pattern is there, then preg_match () will count zero value.

```php
<?php
// create a string
$string = 'abcdefghijklmnopqrstuvwxyz0123456789';

/* preg_match() will find the pattern "abc" in variable $string */
echo preg_match("/abc/", $string);
?>
```

Example 12.2 Pattern Match for beginning of a string

Here the program will check the string "abc" in the beginning.
The regular expression character i.e. regex character for beginning is the caret(^)

```php
<?php
// create a string
$string = 'abcdefghijklmnopqrstuvwxyz0123456789';

// try to match the beginning of the string

if(preg_match("/^abc/", $string))
    {
// if preg_match()function matches the string at the beginning ,then line echoes that "string begins with abc"

    echo 'The string begins with abc';
    }
else
    {
 // if no match is found, then echo this line
    echo 'No match found';
    }
?>
```

The forward slashes are a delimiter that holds regex pattern.

Example 12.3 Pattern Match forinsensitive cases:

If we run the example 12.2 for finding the pattern ABC in regular expression by preg_match(), then it will not be able to find the same because the sear above example is case sensitive and for case in-sensitive, there is need to modifier.

Here, 'i' is used where searching is case-insensitive.

```php
<?php
// create a string
$string = 'abcdefghijklmnopqrstuvwxyz0123456789';

// try to match pattern. Here "i" is used in the syntax for searching of a case-insensitive patterns
if (preg_match ("/^ABC/i", $string))
    {

    echo 'The string begins with abc';
    }
else
    {
    echo 'No match found';
    }
?>
```

Example 12.4 Pattern Match for insensitive cases at the end of a string:

Here the program will find the pattern at the end of the string.

The regular expression character i.e. regex character for pattern matching of a string at the end is to use (\z) and "i" for finding in-sensitive cases.

```php
<?php
// create a string
$string = 'abcdefghijklmnopqrstuvwxyz0123456789';

// try to match pattern at the end of the string
if(preg_match("/89\z/i", $string))
    {
    // if pattern matches then it will echo this
    echo 'The string ends with 89';
    }
else
    {
    // if no match is found then it will echo this line
    echo 'No match found';
    }
```

12.2 PDO

PHP Data Objects and they are used to access databases.

PDO is just like Data Access Layer which provides a uniform method of access to multiple databases.

PHP Data Objects provide methods for prepared statements **which prevent the databases from SQL injection attacks**. The Prepared Statements are precompiled SQL statements that can be executed multiple times by sending just the data to the server.

PDO is a class which consists of the PDOStatement classes like:
PDOStatement::bindColumn which binds a column to a PHP variable.
PDOStatement::bindParam which binds a parameter to the specified variable name.
PDOStatement::bindValue which binds a value to a parameter.
PDOStatement::execute which executes a prepared statement.

Example 12.5 PHP Data Objects for inserting records into database

```php
<?php
$dbhost   = "localhost";
 $dbname  = "pdo";
 $dbuser  = "root";
$dbpass   = "";
$conn = new PDO("mysql:host=$dbhost;dbname=$dbname",$dbuser,$dbpass);
$title = 'PHP Book';
$author = 'Pratiyush Guleria';
$sql = "INSERT INTO books (title,author) VALUES (:title,:author)";
$q = $conn->prepare($sql); $q->execute(array(':author'=>$author,':title'=>
$title));
 ?>
```

Example 12.6. Example of PHP Data Objects for inserting records into database by using classes and objects

Here, Database class is inheriting the PDO class.
The name of database is "doblog" and tablename is "posts".
Attributes taken for this example is: "title", "message", "time".

"connect.inc"

```php
<?php

class DB extends PDO
```

```php
{

/* constructor is defined taking database as the parameter */
/* Databasename is "doblog"
   public function __construct($dbname = "doblog")
   {

/* Here PDO class will raise exception if any exceptional errors are there */
$opt = array(PDO::ATTR_ERRMODE => PDO::ERRMODE_EXCEPTION);
$datasource = "mysql:host=localhost;dbname=$dbname;charset=utf8";
     parent::__construct($datasource, "root", "", $opt);
   }
}
?>
```

PDO::__construct willcreate a PDO instance representing a connection to a database

"post.php"

```php
<?php

/* require statement is used to include the database configuration file "connect.inc" */
   require 'connect.inc.php';
   if( isset($_POST['title'], $_POST['message']) ) {
      $db = new DB('doblog');
/* Here preparedstatement to insert records into database is used */
$stmt = $db->prepare("INSERT INTO posts (title, message, time) VALUES (:title, :message,
:time)");

/*binds a parameter to the specified variable name.*/
$stmt->bindParam(':title', $_POST['title']);
     $stmt->bindParam(':message', $_POST['message']);
     $stmt->bindParam(':time', $time);
     $title = $_POST['title'];
     $message = $_POST['message'];
/*PDOStatement::execute executes a prepared statement*/
     $stmt->execute();
   }
?>
```

"pdo.html"

```html
<html>
<head>
<title>Create blog post</title>
</head>
<body>
```

```html
<form id="add_post" method="post" action= "post.php">
<fieldset>
<legend>Send some message</legend>
<label for="post_title">Title:
<input id="title" type="text" name="title" value="<?php if (isset($title))
{ echo htmlentities ($title);
} ?>"
>
</label>
<label for="message">Message:
<textarea   id="message"   name="message"   rows="20"   cols="30"   maxlength="50"
value="<?php if (isset($message)) { echo htmlentities ($message); } ?>" ></textarea>
</label>
</fieldset>
<input id="send" type="submit" value="Send">
</form>
</div>
</body>
</html>
```

APPENDIX-A

Sample Projects

Sample Project #1. Photogallery

Objective of Project: In this project, images can be uploaded into database along with caption and images can be fetched from the database. The snapshot of file upload is shown in Fig.1

Fig.1: File Upload Control

In order to run this project, perform the following steps:

Create a Database with name = "photoupload".

Create a table with name = "photos".

Create three fields along with their datatypes and size as mentioned i.e. id int(11) location(varchar,5000),caption(varchar,50).

Create a folder with name "photogallery"in C:\wamp\www\ and save all the files mentioned below inside it. Apart from it, create a blank subfolder "photos" inside "photogallery" folder. Please note that "photos" folder name is case-sensitive to run the program

"config.php":

This file is the configuration file containing the configuration of database, localhost, username and password. This file will be required in multiple programs and this config.php file will be called in other files using include statement which is discussed earlier.

```php
<?php
$mysql_hostname = "localhost";
$mysql_user = "root";
$mysql_password = "";
$mysql_database = "photoupload";
$prefix = "";
$bd = mysql_connect($mysql_hostname, $mysql_user, $mysql_password) or die("Could not connect database");
mysql_select_db($mysql_database, $bd) or die("Could not select database");
?>
```

"index.php"

This is the index file where we will browse the image and enter the caption through form and on submit button, next page i.e. "add.php" will execute.

Here in this program, **enctype attribute specifies the way the form data should be encoded when submitting it to the server.**

The multipart/form-data is one of the values of enctype attribute which is used in form element that have a file upload. The multi-part divides form data into multiple parts and sends to server.

```
/* Here, enctype attribute specifies the way the form data should be encoded when submitting
it to the server.
multipart/form-data is one of the values of enctype attribute which is used in form element that
have a file upload. The multi-part divides form data into multiple parts and send to server. */

<form action="add.php" method="post" enctype="multipart/form-data" name="a1">
 Select Picture: <br />
/* First parameter name is "image" which is to be passed in "add.php" file  */
<input type="file" name="image"><br />
Enter the Caption<br />
/* Second Parameter name is "caption" which is to be passed in "add.php"
file*/ <input name="caption" type="text"/>
<br />
<input type="submit" name="Submit" value="Upload Picture" id="button1" /> </
form>
<br />
Pictures Displayed
<br />
<br />
<?php

error_reporting(0);
/* config.php file mentioned above is included into this file for database configurations */
include('config.php');

/* Using SELECT query,all pics are fetched from table */

$result = mysql_query("SELECT * FROM photos");
while($row = mysql_fetch_array($result))
{
echo '<p><img src="'.$row['location'].'"></p>';
echo '<p>'.$row['caption'].' </p>';
}
?>
```

"add.php"

The $_FILES is a super global variable which will contain all the uploaded file information.

In this file, a PHP script isused with a HTML form to allow users to upload files to the server. The files are initially uploaded into a temporary directory i.e. "tmp_name" and then relocated to a target destination by a PHP script.

The files uploaded by the user will be saved in the database as well as in the photos folder which we have created in **C:\wamp\www\photogallery\photos because in database the location field will show the path of file as /photos/sunflower.jpg.**

```php
<?php

/* config.php file mentioned above is included into this file for database configurations */

include('config.php');
if (!isset($_FILES['image']['tmp_name'])) {
        echo "";
        }else{

/* Here move_uploaded_file() function is used to upload files to the
server. The files are uploaded in the temporary directory and from there, it
will move from "/photos/" folder in "C:\wamp\www\photogallery\" to database. */
move_uploaded_file($_FILES[" image" ][" tmp_name" ]," photos/".
$_FILES["image"]["name"]);

                $location="photos/" . $_FILES["image"]["name"];
                $caption=$_POST['caption'];

                $save=mysql_query("INSERT INTO photos (location, caption)
VALUES ('$location','$caption')");

/* Here, header is used to open the window i.e. "index.php" file to view the files fetched from
database */

                header("location: index.php");
                exit();
        }
?>
```

Sample Project #2. Registration Form and Databases

In this project, records will be inserted using Registration Form shown in Fig.2 and after inserting the records into database, these records can be retrieved from the database.
This project is simple one and guides the students to insert and read records from

database following simple programming stuff.

Fig.2: Registration Form Snapshot

"applicationform.hml"

```html
<html>
<head>
</head>
<title>Registration Form</title>
<body>
<div align="center">

<h1>REGISTRATION FORM</h1>
<br />

<form action = "registration_form.php" method = "post">

1.COURSE NO. <input type = text name = "courseno"><br/>
2.ROLL NO. <input type = text name = "rollno">
<br />
3.NAME(Mr./Ms.)<input type = text name = "name"><br/>
4.FATHER'S NAME(Sh.)<input type = text name = "fathername">
<br />
5.DATE OF BIRTH.:<select name = "Day">
<option value="Select">Select</option>
<option value="1">1</option>
<option value="2">2</option>
<option value="3">3</option>
<option value="4">4</option>
<option value="5">5</option>
<option value="6">6</option>
```

```html
<option value="7">7</option>
<option value="8">8</option>
<option value="9">9</option>
<option value="10">10</option>
<option value="11">11</option>
<option value="12">12</option>
<option value="13">13</option>
<option value="14">14</option>
<option value="15">15</option>
<option value="16">16</option>
<option value="17">17</option>
<option value="18">18</option>
<option value="19">19</option>
<option value="20">20</option>
<option value="21">21</option>
<option value="22">22</option>
<option value="23">23</option>
<option value="24">24</option>
<option value="25">25</option>
<option value="26">26</option>
<option value="27">27</option>
<option value="28">28</option>
<option value="29">29</option>
<option value="30">30</option>
<option value="31">31</option>
</select>
<select name="Month">
<option value="Month">Month</option>
<option value="JAN">JAN</option>
<option value="FEB">FEB</option>
<option value="MAR">MAR</option>
<option value="ARL">ARL</option>
<option value="MAY">MAY</option>
<option value="JUN">JUN</option>
<option value="JUL">JUL</option>
<option value="AUG">AUG</option>
<option value="SEP">SEP</option>
<option value="OCT">OCT</option>
<option value="NOV">NOV</option>
<option value="DEC">DEC</option>
</select>
<select name="Year">
<option value="Year" selected>Year</option>
<option value="1980">1980</option>
<option value="1981">1981</option>
```

```
<option value="1982">1982</option>
<option value="1983">1983</option>
<option value="1984">1984</option>
<option value="1985">1985</option>
<option value="1986">1986</option>
<option value="1987">1987</option>
<option value="1988">1988</option>
<option value="1989">1989</option>
<option value="1990">1990</option>
<option value="1991">1991</option>
<option value="1992">1992</option>
<option value="1993">1993</option>
<option value="1994">1994</option>
<option value="1995">1995</option>
<option value="1996">1996</option>
<option value="1997">1997</option>
<option value="1998">1998</option>
<option value="1999">1999</option>
<option value="2000">2000</option>
<option value="2001">2001</option>
<option value="2002">2002</option>
<option value="2003">2003</option>
<option value="2004">2004</option>
<option value="2005">2005</option>
<option value="2006">2006</option>
<option value="2007">2007</option>
<option value="2008">2008</option>
<option value="2009">2009</option>
<option value="2010">2010</option>
 <option value="2011">2011</option>
<option value="2012">2012</option>
<option value="2013">2013</option>
<option value="2014">2014</option>
<option value="2015">2015</option>
<option value="2016">2016</option>
<option value="2017">2017</option>
<option value="2018">2018</option>
</select>
<br />
6. SEXCODE.:
<input name = "gender" type = radio value = "Male" checked>Male
<input name = "gender" type = radio value = "Female">Female
<br/>
7. QUALIFICATION:
<select name = "Qual">
<option value="Select" selected>Select</option>
```

```
<option value="BCA">BCA</option>
<option value="MCA">MCA</option>
<option value="PGDCA">PGDCA</option>
<option value="DCA">DCA</option>
</select>
<br />
ADDRESS:
<br>
<textarea cols = 60 rows = 10 name = "Address"></textarea>

<input type="submit" value = "submit">
<br/>
</form>
</div>
</body>
</html>
```

"registration_form.php"
In order to run this program, please follow the steps:
       Create a database with name **"register"** and tablename **"reg"**.
       Create following attributes with data type varchar for all these fields:

"course,rollno,name,fathername,Day,Month,Year,gender,Qual,Address"

```
<?php
$con=mysql_connect ("localhost","root","");
if(!$con)
{
die('could not connect:'.mysql_error());
}
mysql_select_db ("register",$con);
$sql = "INSERT INTO reg(course,rollno,name,fathername,Day,Month,Year,gen-
der,Qual,Address)
values('$_POST[courseno]','$_POST[rollno]','$_POST[name]','$_-
POST[fathername]','$_POST[Day]','$_POST[Month]','$_POST[Year]','$_POST[gender]',
'$_POST[Qual]','$_POST[Address]')";

if(!mysql_query($sql,$con))
{
die('Error:'.mysql_error());
}

echo "1 Record Added";
mysql_close($con);
?>
<html>
```

```
<head></head>
<title></title>
<body>
<a href = "read.php">Click me to view the records</a>
</body>
</html>
```

"read.php"

```php
<?php
mysql_connect("localhost","root","");
mysql_select_db("register");
$result = mysql_query("SELECT * FROM reg");
if($result && mysql_num_rows($result))
{
  $numrows = mysql_num_rows($result);
  $rowcount = 1;
print "There are $numrows people registered in database:<br/><br/>";

  while($row = mysql_fetch_assoc($result))
{
 print "Row $rowcount<br/>";
 foreach($row as $var => $val)
{
 print "<B>$var</B>:$val<br/>";
 }
print "<br/>";
++$rowcount;
}
}
?>
```

Sample Project #3. Sessions using databases

In this project, username and password will be checked in the database and accordingly session will be maintained.

In order to run the program, please go through the database structure defined:

```
CREATE DATABASE test;
CREATE TABLE login (
id int(10) NOT NULL AUTO_INCREMENT,
username varchar(255) NOT NULL,
password varchar(255) NOT NULL,
PRIMARY KEY (id)
)
```

In this example, cascading style sheet is used to give look and feel to the form designed in multiple pages.

Use this style sheet in every PHP script page so that the elements, classes defined in the style sheets can be used in the PHP script pages.

"style.css"

```
/* Here id is defined with "#".These id are used in the programs using div tag */

#main {
width:860px;
margin:40px auto;
font-family:Calibri
}
span {
color:red
}
h2 {
background-color:#FEFFED;
text-align:center;
border-radius:9px 9px 0 0;
margin:-10px -40px;
padding:10px
}
hr {
border:0;
border-bottom:1px solid #ccc;
margin:10px -40px;
margin-bottom:30px
}
#login {
width:250px;
float:left;
border-radius:9px;
font-family:Calibri;
border:2px solid #ccc;
padding:10px 40px 25px;
margin-top:50px
}
input[type=text],input[type=password] {
width:99%;
padding:9px;
margin-top:8px;
border:1px solid #ccc;
padding-left:5px;
```

```css
font-size:16px;
font-family:raleway
}
input[type=submit] {
width:100%;
background-color:#FFBC00;
color:#fff;
border:2px solid #FFCB00;
padding:10px;
font-size:18px;
cursor:pointer;
border-radius:5px;
margin-bottom:15px
}
#profile {
padding:30px;
font-size:20px;
background-color:#DCE6F7
}
#logout {
float:right;
padding:5px;
}
a {
text-decoration:none;
color:#6495ed
}
i {
color:#6495ed
}
```

"index.php"

```php
<?php
include('login.php'); // Includes Login Script

if(isset($_SESSION['login_user'])){
header("location: profile.php");
}
?>
<html>
<head>
<title>Login Form in PHP with Session</title>
/* Here CSS is referred */
<link href="style.css" rel="stylesheet" type="text/css">
```

```
</head>
<body>
<div id="main">
<h1>PHP Login Session Example</h1>
<div id="login">
<h2>Login Form</h2>
<form action="" method="post">
<label>UserName :</label>
<input id="name" name="username" placeholder="username" type="text">
<label>Password :</label>
<input id="password" name="password" placeholder="**********" type="password">
<input name="submit" type="submit" value=" Login ">
<span> <?php echo $error; ?> </span>
</form>
</div>
</div>
</body>
</html>
```

"login.php"

```
<?php
session_start(); // Starting Session
$error=''; // Variable To Store Error Message
if (isset($_POST['submit'])) {
if (empty($_POST['username']) || empty($_POST['password'])) {
$error = "Username or Password is invalid";
}
else
{
// Define $username and $password
$username=$_POST['username'];
$password=$_POST['password'];
// Establishing Connection with Server by passing server_name, user_id and password as a
parameter
$connection = mysql_connect("localhost", "root", "");
// To protect MySQL injection for Security purpose
$username = stripslashes($username);
$password = stripslashes($password);
$username = mysql_real_escape_string($username);
$password = mysql_real_escape_string($password);
// Selecting Database
$db = mysql_select_db("test", $connection);
// SQL query to fetch information of registerd users and finds user match.
$query = mysql_query("select * from login where password='$password' AND
username='$username'", $connection);
```

```php
$rows = mysql_num_rows($query);
if ($rows == 1) {
$_SESSION['login_user']=$username; // Initializing Session
header("location: profile.php"); // Redirecting To Other Page
} else {
$error = "Username or Password is invalid";
}
mysql_close($connection); // Closing Connection
}
}
?>
```

"session.php"

> In this page, the session is maintained and it is checked whether the session is stored in the variable or not. This "session.php" file is being included into "profile.php" page.

```php
<?php
/* Establishing Connection with Server by passing servername, userid and password as a parameter */
$connection = mysql_connect("localhost", "root", "");
// Selecting Database
$db = mysql_select_db("test", $connection);
session_start();// Starting Session
// Storing Session
$user_check=$_SESSION['login_user'];
// SQL Query To Fetch Complete Information Of User
$sql=mysql_query("select username from login where username='$user_check'", $connection);
$row = mysql_fetch_assoc($sql);
$login_session =$row['username'];
if(!isset($login_session)){
mysql_close($connection); // Closing Connection
header('Location: index.php'); // Redirecting To Home Page
}
?>
```

"profile.php"

```php
<?php
include('session.php');
?>

<html>
<head>
<title>Your Home Page</title>
<link href="style.css" rel="stylesheet" type="text/css">
```

```
</head>
<body>
<div id="profile">
<b id="welcome">Welcome : <i><?php echo $login_session; ?></i></b>
<b id="logout"><a href="logout.php">Log Out</a></b>
</div>
</body>
</html>
```

"logout.php"

```
<?php
session_start();
if(session_destroy()) // Destroying All Sessions
{
header("Location: index.php"); // Redirecting To Home Page
}
?>
```

Sample Project #4. Students Course Registration

In this project, records will be inserted by using web pageas shown in Fig.4 and after inserting the records into database, these records can be retrieved from the database as well they can be searched.

This project is simple one and guides the students to read, insert, delete, update and search records from database following simple programming stuff.

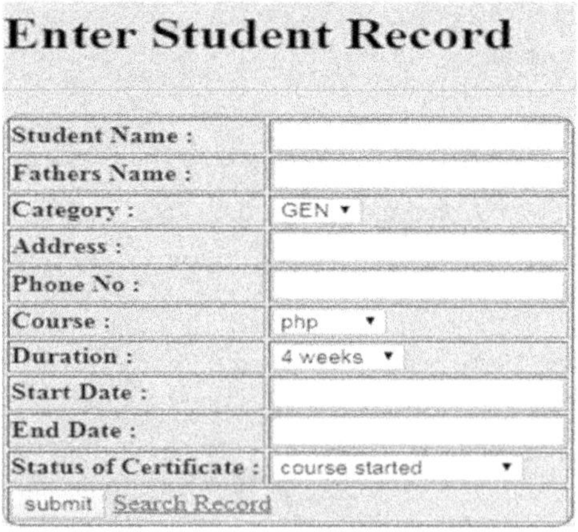

Fig.4: Student Record Management

"record_test.html"

```
<html>
```

```
<head>
<title>e-form</title>
</head>
<body>
<h1>Enter Student Record</h1>
<hr></hr>
<form method="POST" action="record2.php">
<p>
<table border="1px">
<tr>
<th>Student Name : </th>
<td><input type="text" name="sname"></td>
</tr>
<tr>
<th>Fathers Name : </th>
<td><input type="text" name="fname"></td>
</tr>
<tr>
<th>Category : <th>

<select name="category">
<option value="GEN">GEN</option>
<option value="ST">ST</option>
<option value="SC">SC</option>
</select>

</tr>
<tr>
<th>Address : </th>
<td><input type="text" name="address"></td>
</tr>
<tr>
<th>Phone No : </th>
<td><input type="text" name="phone"></td>
</tr>
<tr>
<th>Course : <th>
<select name="course">
<option value="php">php</option>
<option value="java">java</option>
<option value="asp.net">asp.net</option>
</select>
</tr>
<tr>
<th>Duration : <th>
```

```html
<select name="duration">
<option value="4weeks">4 weeks</option>
<option value="6weeks">6 weeks</option>
<option value="6months">6 months</option>
</select>
</tr>
<tr>
<th>Start Date : </th>
<td>
```

/* Here datetimepickers can be used using jqueries */

```html
<input type="text" name="sdate"></td>
</tr>
<tr>
<th>End Date : </th>
<td>
<input type="text" name="edate">
</td>
</tr>
<tr>
<th>Status of Certificate : </th>
<td>
<select name="cert_status">
<option value="coursestarted">course started</option>
<option value="courserunning">course running</option>
<option value="awardlistsend">awardlist submitted</option>
<option value="awardlistpending">awardlist pending</option>
<option value="provisionalcertificate">provisional certificate</option>
<option value="testnotgiven">test not given</option>
</select>
</td>
</tr>

<tr>
<td colspan="2"><input type="submit" value="submit" name="submit">
<a href="search.html">Search Record</a>
</td>
</tr>
</table>
</p>
</form>
</body>
</html>
```

"record2.php"

```
<html>
<head>
<title></title>
</head>
<body>
<?php
$con=mysql_connect("localhost","root","");
if(!$con)
{
die('could not connect'.mysql_error());
}
mysql_select_db("record",$con);

$sql="insert into
srecord(student_name,father_name,category,address,
mobile_no,course,duration,start_date,end_date,cert_status) values ('$_POST[sname]','$_POST
[fname]','$_POST[category]','$_POST[address]','$_POST[-
phone]','$_POST[course]','$_POST[duration]','$_POST[sdate]','$_POST[edate]','$_POST[cert_st
atus]')";

if(!mysql_query($sql,$con))
{
die('error:'.mysql_error());
}
echo"Record Added !";
echo"<p><a href="record.html">Return To Main Page</a></p>";
mysql_close($con);
?>
</body>
</html>
```

"search.html"

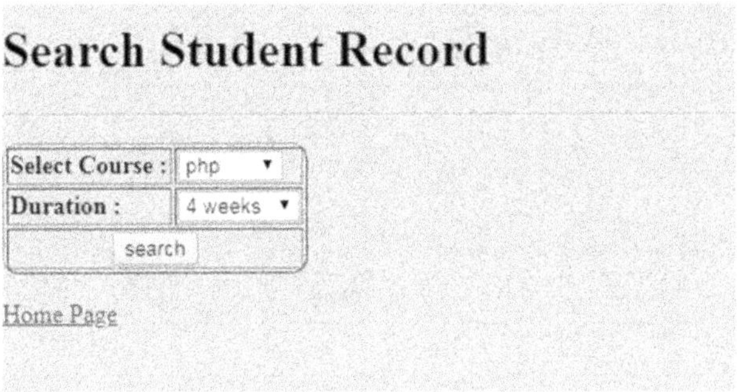

Fig.5: Search Record

```html
<html>
<head>
<title>search form</title>
</head>
<body>
<h1>Search Student Record</h1>
<hr></hr>
<form method="POST" action="record3.php">
<p>
<table border="1px">
<tr>
<th>Select Course : <th>
<select name="course">
<option value="php">php</option>
<option value="java">java</option>
<option value="asp.net">asp.net</option>
</select>
</tr>

<tr>
<th>Duration : <th>
<select name="duration">
<option value="4weeks">4 weeks</option>
<option value="6weeks">6 weeks</option>
<option value="6months">6 months</option>
</select>
</tr>
<tr>
<td colspan="2" align="center"><input type="submit" value="search" name="submit"></td>
</tr>
</table>
</p>
</form>
<a href="record.html">Home Page</a>
</body>
</html>
```

"record3.php"

```php
<?php

$con=mysql_connect("localhost","root","");
if(!$con)
{
die('could not connect'.mysql_error());
}
```

```
mysql_select_db("record",$con);
$sql = "select * from srecord where course='$_POST[course]' and duration='$_POST[dura-
tion]'";
$result=mysql_query($sql,$con);
print"<table width='700' border='1'>";
print"<tr><th>Student ID</th><th>Student Name</th><th>Fathers Name</
th><th>Cat- egory</th><th>Address</th><th>Phone No</th><th>Course</
th><th>Dura- tion</th><th>Start Date</th><th>End Date</th></tr>";
while($row=mysql_fetch_array($result))
{
print" <tr><td> ".$row[0]." </td><td> ".$row[1]." </td><td> ".$row[2]." </
td><td> ".$row[3]." </td><td> ".$row[4]." </td><td> ".$row[5]." </td><td> ".$row[6]."
</td><td> ".$row[7]." </td><td> ".$row[8]." </td><td> ".$row[9]." </td><tr>";
}
print"</table>";
echo '<a href="record.html">Home Page</a>';
mysql_close($con);
?>
```

Sample Project #5. Update and Delete operations

The sample snapshot of the program is shown in Fig.6

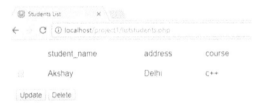

Fig.6:Display Screen

In order to run this project, create the following database structure:
CREATE DATABASE **record;**
CREATE TABLE **student**
Attributes: studentid varchar(10) NOT NULL
student_name varchar(40) NOT NULL
address varchar(50) NOT NULL,
course varchar(50) NOT NULL
PRIMARY KEY (studentid)
)

"sample.js"

> This file is a JavaScript file and in this file, two functions are created, one is for update and other is for delete operation.

```
function setUpdateAction() {
document.frmUser.action = "update.php";
```

```
document.frmUser.submit();
}
function setDeleteAction() {
if(confirm("Are you sure want to delete these rows?")) {
document.frmUser.action = "delete.php";
document.frmUser.submit();
}
}
```

"styles.css"

Here cascading style sheet is used and classes are defined inside it once and used in multiple pages to avoid repetition and provide look and feel to web pages.

```
body {
font-family:Arial;
}
input {
font-family:Arial;
font-size:14px;
}
label{
font-family:Arial;
font-size:14px;
color:#999999;
}
.tblSaveForm {
border-top:2px #999999 solid;
background-color: #f8f8f8;
}
.tableheader {
background-color: #fedc4d;
}
.tablerow {
background-color: #A7D6F1;
color:white;
}
.btnSubmit {
background-color:#fd9512;
padding:5px;
border-color:#FF6600;
border-radius:4px;
color:white;
}
.message {
color: #FF0000;
```

```css
text-align: center;
width: 100%;
}
.txtField {
padding: 5px;
border:#fedc4d 1px solid;
border-radius:4px;
}
.evenRow {
background-color: #E2EDF9;
font-size:12px;
color:#101010;
}
.evenRow:hover {
background-color: #ffef46;
}
.oddRow {
background-color: #B3E8FF;
font-size:12px;
color:#101010;
}
.oddRow:hover {
background-color: #ffef46;
}
.tblListForm {
border-top:2px #999999 solid;
}
.listheader {
background-color: #fedc4d;
font-size:12px;
font-weight:bold;
}
```

"liststudents.php"

In this program, classes and elements defined in "styles.css" file are used for accessing the properties.

```php
<?php
error_reporting(0);
$conn = mysql_connect("localhost","root","");
mysql_select_db("record",$conn);
$result = mysql_query("SELECT * FROM student");
?>
<html>
<head>
<title>Student List</title>
<link rel="stylesheet" type="text/css" href="styles.css" />
```

```
<script language="JavaScript" src="sample.js" type="text/JavaScript"></script>
</head>
<body>
<form name="frmUser" method="post" action="">
<div style="width:500px;">
<table border="0" cellpadding="10" cellspacing="1" width="500" class="tblListForm">
<tr class="listheader">
<td></td>
<td>student_name</td>
<td>address</td>
<td>course</td>
</tr>
<?php
$i=0;
while($row = mysql_fetch_array($result)) {
if($i%2==0)
$classname="evenRow";
else
$classname="oddRow";
?>
<tr class="<?php if(isset($classname)) echo $classname;?>">
<td><input type="checkbox" name="users[]" value="<?php echo $row["studentid"]; ?>"
></td>
<td><?php echo $row["student_name"]; ?></td>
<td><?php echo $row["address"]; ?></td>
<td><?php echo $row["course"]; ?></td>
</tr>
<?php
$i++;
}
?>
<tr class="listheader">
<td colspan="4">
/* Here the setUpdateAction() and setDeleteAction() functions are called from the
"sample.js" file */
<input type="button" name="update" value="Update" onClick="setUpdateAction();" /><input type="button" name="delete" value="Delete"  onClick="setDeleteAction();" /></td>
</tr>
</table>
</form>
</div>
</body></html>
```

"update.php"

```
<?php
```

```php
error_reporting(0);
$conn = mysql_connect("localhost","root","");
mysql_select_db("record",$conn);

if(isset($_POST["submit"]) && $_POST["submit"]!="") {
$usersCount = count($_POST["student_name"]);
for($i=0;$i<$usersCount;$i++) {

mysql_query("UPDATE student set student_name='" . $_POST["student_name"][$i] . "',
address='" . $_POST["address"][$i] . "', course='" . $_POST["course"][$i]. "' where studentid =
".$_POST["studentid"][$i]."");

}
header("Location:liststudents.php");
}
?>
<html>
<head>
<title>Edit Record</title>
<link rel="stylesheet" type="text/css" href="styles.css" />
</head>
<body>
<form name="frmUser" method="post" action="">
<div style="width:500px;">
<table border="0" cellpadding="10" cellspacing="0" width="500" align="center">
<tr class="tableheader">
<td>Edit Record</td>
</tr>
<?php
$rowCount = count($_POST["users"]);
for($i=0;$i<$rowCount;$i++) {
$result = mysql_query("SELECT * FROM student WHERE studentid=" . $_POST["users"][$i] . "");
$row[$i]= mysql_fetch_array($result);
?>
<tr>
<td>
<table border="0" cellpadding="10" cellspacing="0" width="500" align="center" class="tbl-
SaveForm">
<tr>
<td><label>Student Name</label></td>
<td><input type="hidden" name="studentid[]" class="txtField" value="<?php echo
$row[$i]['studentid']; ?>"><input type="text" name="student_name[]" class="txtField"
value="<?php echo $row[$i]['student_name']; ?>"></td>
</tr>
<tr>
<td><label>Address</label></td>
```

```
<td><input type="text" name="address[]" class="txtField" value="<?php echo $row[$i]['ad-
dress']; ?>"></td>
</tr>
<td><label>Course</label></td>
<td><input    type="text"    name="course[]"    class="txtField"    value="<?php    echo
$row[$i]['course']; ?>"></td>
</tr>

</table>
</td>
</tr>
<?php
}
?>
<tr>
<td colspan="2"><input type="submit" name="submit" value="Submit" class="btnSub-
mit"></td>
</tr>
</table>
</div>
</form>
</body></html>
```

"delete.php"

```
<?php
$conn = mysql_connect("localhost","root","");
mysql_select_db("record",$conn);
$rowCount = count($_POST["users"]);
for($i=0;$i<$rowCount;$i++) {
mysql_query("DELETE FROM student WHERE studentid='" . $_POST["users"][$i] . "'");
}
header("Location:liststudents.php");
?>
```

Sample Practice Paper-I

SECTION I

A)Answer the following multiple choice questions:

Note: For each question, four choices are given, out of which one Choice is correct. You are required to fill correct choice in ( )

1. What does PHP stands for:
a) Personal Hypertext Processor
b) PHP: Hypertext Preprocessor
c) Private Home Page
d) Personal Home Page

2. PHP server scripts are surrounded by delimiters, which?
a) <? php?>
b) <&>...</&>
c) <? php>...</?>
d) <script>...</script>

3. How do you write "Hello World" in PHP?
a) "Hello World";
b) Document. Write ("Hello World");
c) echo "Hello World";
d) All of the above

4. All variables in PHP start with which symbol?
a) !
b) $
c) &
d) None

5. What is the correct way to end a PHP statement?
a);
b).
c) </php>
d) New Line

6. Which one of the following is used to see the calendar of current month?
a) cal
b) calc
c) date
d) none of above

7. What is output of $arrnew = array_merge($array1,$array2):
a) will add contents
b) give an error
c) $arrnew will contain array1 & array2
d) none of above

8. To receive value from a form:
a) $_REQUIRE
b) $_POST
c) $_GET
d) all of the above

9. The include statement allows you to include and attach other PHP scripts to your own script.
a) True
b) false

10. What does isset ($var) do?
a) If $var has a value other than the empty set (0), an empty string, or NULL.
b)If $var has any value other than NULL, including the empty set or an empty string.

c) None of these

B) **State which of the following is true or false:**

1. MySQL is a relational database management system.
2. When using the POST method, variables are displayed in the URL.
3. In PHP, you can use both single quotes ('') and double quotes ("") for strings.
4. Include files must have the file extension ".inc".
5. Foreach loop displays all the values in an array.
6. Apache is a database server in Linux.
7. Mysql_connect is used to select a database from php.
8. Is_array () is an inbuilt function in arrays.
9. PHP allows you to send emails directly from a script.
10. The code to include in the file upload field is <input type = "file" name = "file">.

C) **Match the following:**

1. Array in php	a) multidimensional
2. Which function would you use to return a row from the recordset as an array?	b) $my-var
3. How would you end a session and erase all traces of it for future visits.	c) Contains information from POST requests.
4.variable having illegal name	d) retrieves $array[5], not $array['index'];
5. $_POST[]	e) new
6. define('index',5); echo $array[index];	f) ->
7. To create an object of a given class	g) function defined inside a class
8. to access methods and properties of the object	h) function to check for database support
9. method	i) mysql_fetch_array()
10. The php.ini configuration file has a setting that globally limits the size of file upload.	j) upload_max_filesize
	k) session_destroy()

D) Fill in the blanks:

a) $ b)cookies   c)include() or require()   d) now()   e) session

f) array   g)$_GET   h) $_POST   i) CSS   j)redundant

k) strstr()   l) include_once()   m)mysql_query()   n)grep   o) server-side

1. The _____function searches for a string within another string in PHP.
2. _____are added to HTML to give web developers and users more control over the way their web pages display.
3. An _____ is a special variable, which can store multiple values in one single variable.
4. The processing of PHP on the server is called_ _____processing.
5. You can insert the content of one PHP file into another PHP file before the server executes it, with the _____ or _____ function.
6. _____function returns the current date and time according to the setting of your computer's system date and time.
7. We can track certain user details using_____.
8. To have the database execute the query, use the _____function.
9. Another statement that performs the same function as include () is_____.
10. The First Normal Form involves removal of _____data from horizontal rows.